GW01377078

NORTH Western Australia's

Pilbara and the Kimberley

This book is dedicated to my Mum and Dad, and my brother Adrian

Photographed by Ben Knapinski

2   Jabiru nest boab tree, Karunji Road, El Questro Wilderness Park, East Kimberley

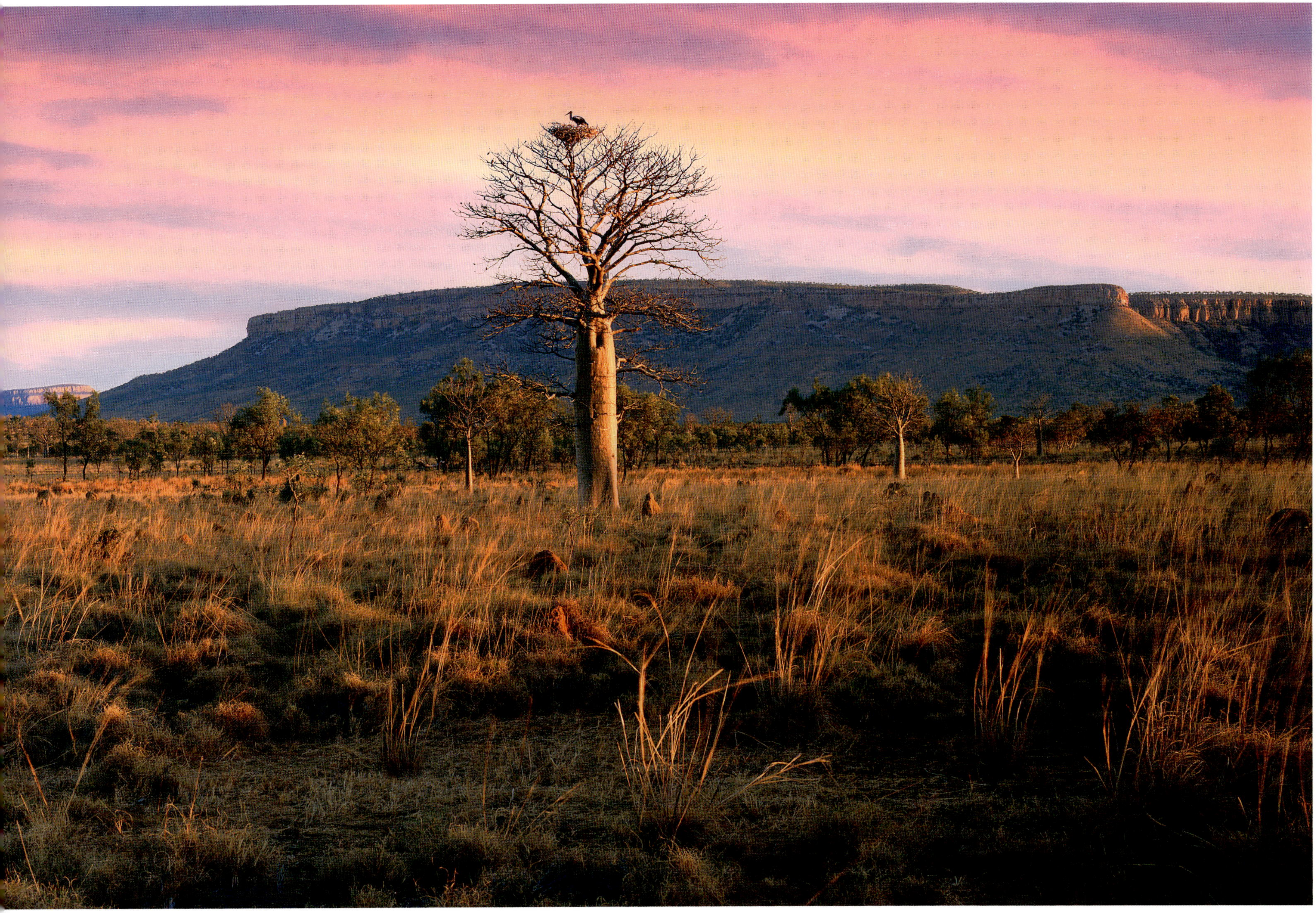

Darwin
Perth
Australia
Port Hedland
Dampier
Wickham
Cossack
Roebourne
Karratha
Whim Creek
Marble Bar
Fortescue River Roadhouse
Millstream Chichester National Park
Yandeyarra
Onslow
Pannawonica
Mungaroona Range Nature Reserve
Exmouth
Mulga Downs
Wittenoom
Mt Brockman
Hamersley Range
Bonney Downs
Auski Roadhouse
Duck Creek
Nanutarra Roadhouse
Mt Bruce
Tom Price
Karijini National Park
Ningaloo
Coral Bay
Paraburdoo
Newman
Capricorn Roadhouse
Minilya Roadhouse
Pilbara
Collier Range National Park
Kumarina Roadhouse
North West Coastal Highway
Great Northern Highway
Marble Bar Road
*Map not to scale

THE PILBARA

The Pilbara spans approximately 500,000 square kilometers of the north-western corner of Australia. Known for its rugged scenery and rock formations dated half as old as the earth, over two billion years old.

There is much to see in the Pilbara. From 80 Mile Beach, to the palm lined oasis of Millstream, to the legendary Whim Creek Pub. There is the historic coastal town of Cossack, Australia's hottest town of Marble Bar, the blow holes of Point Quobba, the Dampier Archipelago of 42 islands, and the Rudall River National Park on the edge of the Great Sandy Desert - arguably the most remote national park in Australia, and much more.

By demand the first section of this book mainly focuses on one of the Pilbara's most popular attractions which is Karijini National Park set in the heart of the Pilbara in the Hamersley Range. In the accessible northern half of the park, the deep shady chasms with cool clear flowing water and rocks with an intense range of fold lines, patterns and colours leave tourists describing it like no place on earth.

Each gorge is very different, some with narrow spiraling speed slide like water ways and plunge pools several meters high. It is no doubt one of the best 'must see' national parks in Australia.

Perhaps Karijini is not for everyone as there can be a lot of climbing and walking involved, often over slippery rocks. Each gorge has varying grades of difficulty so some will be more suitable than others. Guided tours are recommended. For those who are able to do the gorge walks, Karijini will be an experience like no other.

Knox Gorge - Last plunge pool (abseil only)

Darwin
KIMBERLEY
Australia
Perth
Kalumburu
Walsh Point
Kimberley Coastal Camp
Surveyors Pool
Mitchell Falls
King Edward River
King George River
Drysdale River
Kalumburu Road
Drysdale River Station
Wyndham
Home Valley
Jack's Waterhole
Kununurra
Ellenbrae
Emma Gorge
El Questro
Gibb River Road
Lake Argyle Village
Lake Argyle
Pentecost River
Durack River
Chamberlain River
Cape Leveque
Cape Leveque Road
MT Elizabeth
Barnett River Gorge
Manning Gorge
Mt Hart Wilderness Lodge
Beverley Springs
Mt Barnett Road House
Galvin Gorge
Robinson River
Bell Gorge
Silent Grove
Mount House
Lake Argyle Diamond Mine
Meda River
Fraser River
Derby
Lennard River Gorge
Imintji
Windjana Gorge National Park
Tunnel Creek National Park
Mornington Wilderness Camp
Bungle Bungle Range
Broome
Geikie Gorge National Park
Fitzroy Crossing
Fitzroy River
Halls Creek
Great Northern Highway
Kimberley
*Map not to scale

THE KIMBERLEY

The Kimberley region covers over 400,000 square kilometres in the far north of Western Australia and attracts visitors throughout Australia and the world wanting to experience the "great Australian outback".

The major reasons for the tourist influx in the dry season between April and November are attractions such as the internationally renown 'Bungle Bungle' beehive rock formations, along with El Questro Wilderness Park, the white sands of Cable Beach in Broome, and the station and gorge country of the Gibb River Road. Many tourists still visit the major centres of Broome and Kununurra during the spectacular wet season between November and April when much of the landscape changes colour with new growth.

The dry season weather known for its cooler temperatures averages around the high twenties with low humidity. Inland areas at night can sometimes approach freezing. During the wet season it can get higher than 40 degrees Celsius with extreme humidity.

The variety of attractions in the Kimberley can be dazzling. There are many rugged ranges with some made from ancient Devonian reef 350 million years old. There are tidal flats and mud banks and just around the corner you can find bright white shell beaches. There are secluded rainforest pockets, waterfalls and pools scattered throughout what can sometimes appear to be a desolate landscape. An amazing abundance of wildlife can be found with many species unique to the area. Fishing for the mighty Barramundi in rivers and creeks is a highlight for many.

Traces of Aboriginal heritage can be seen dating back tens of thousands of years. Their beautiful rock art greatly intrigues many who discover it and is well respected and protected by the Kimberley locals. It is still unclear who painted the countless number of 'Bradshaw' rock art paintings. They have been dated at least 22,000 years old and are stunning in their elegance and sophistication.

Their is something about the Kimberley that words can not describe. It keeps travellers coming back year after year.... Some never leave.

Windjana Gorge National Park

Kermit's Pool, Hancock Gorge, Karijini N.P.

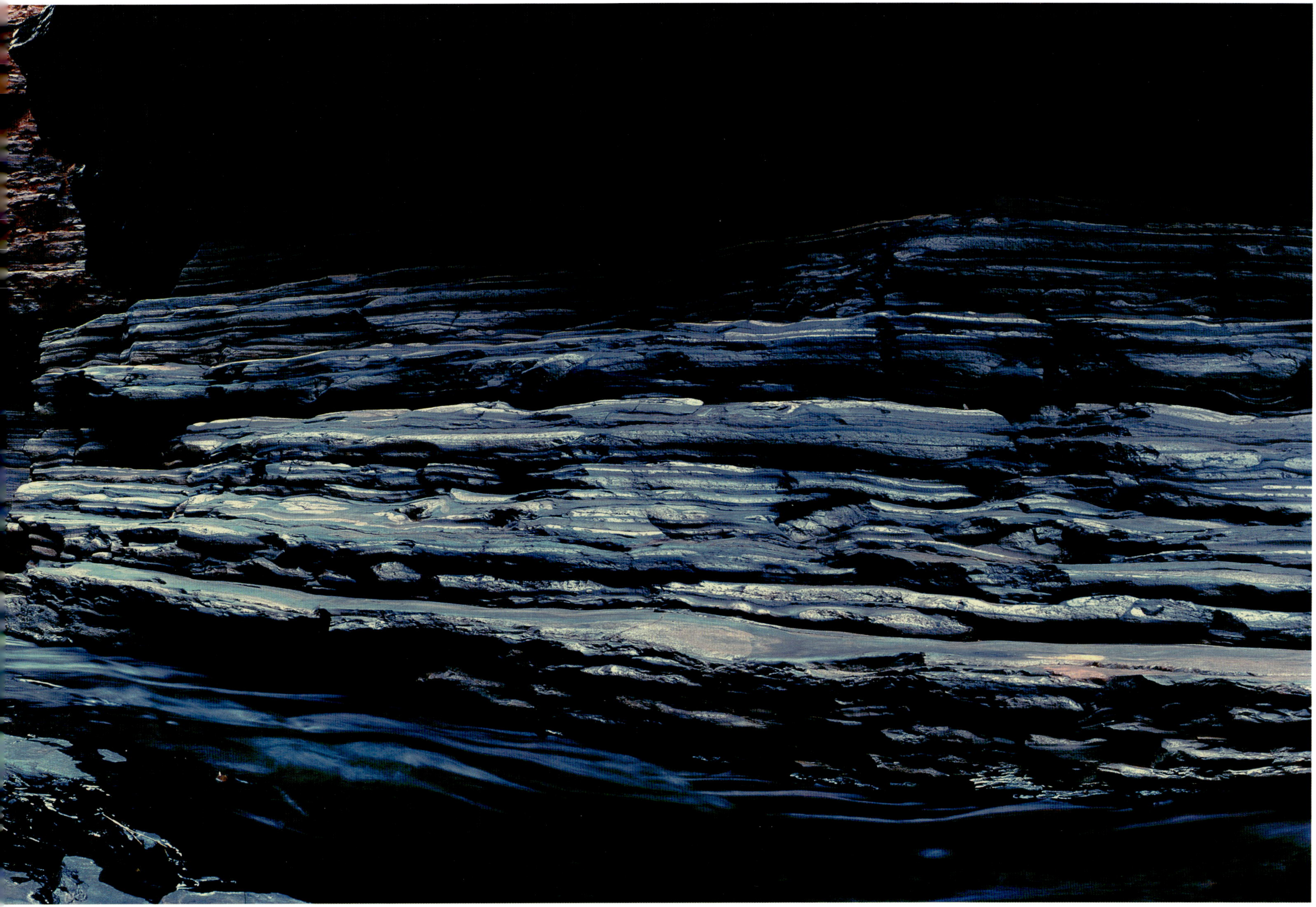

10   Circular Pool, Dales Gorge, Karijini N.P.

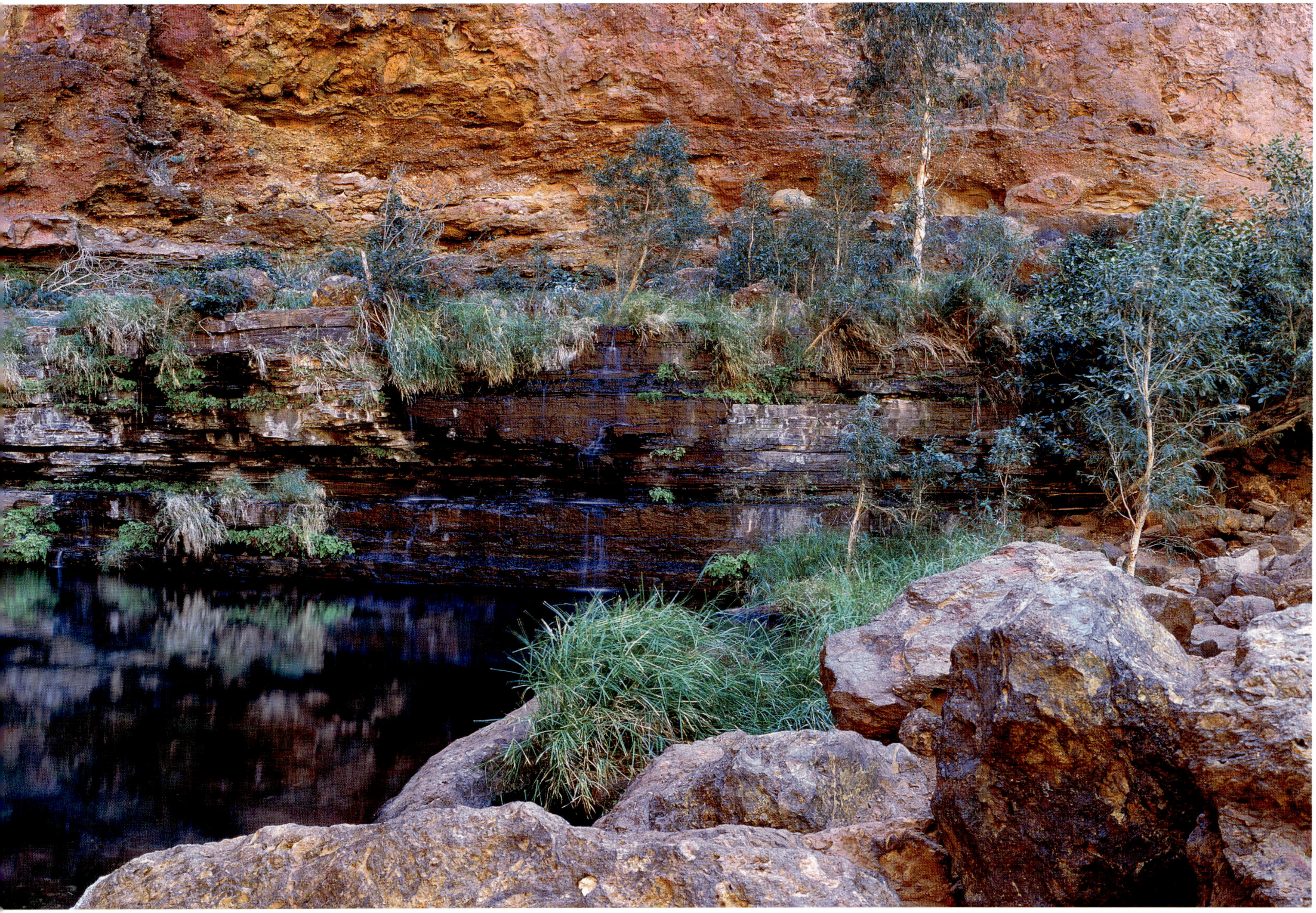

12 Circular Pool ferns, Dales Gorge, Karijini N.P.

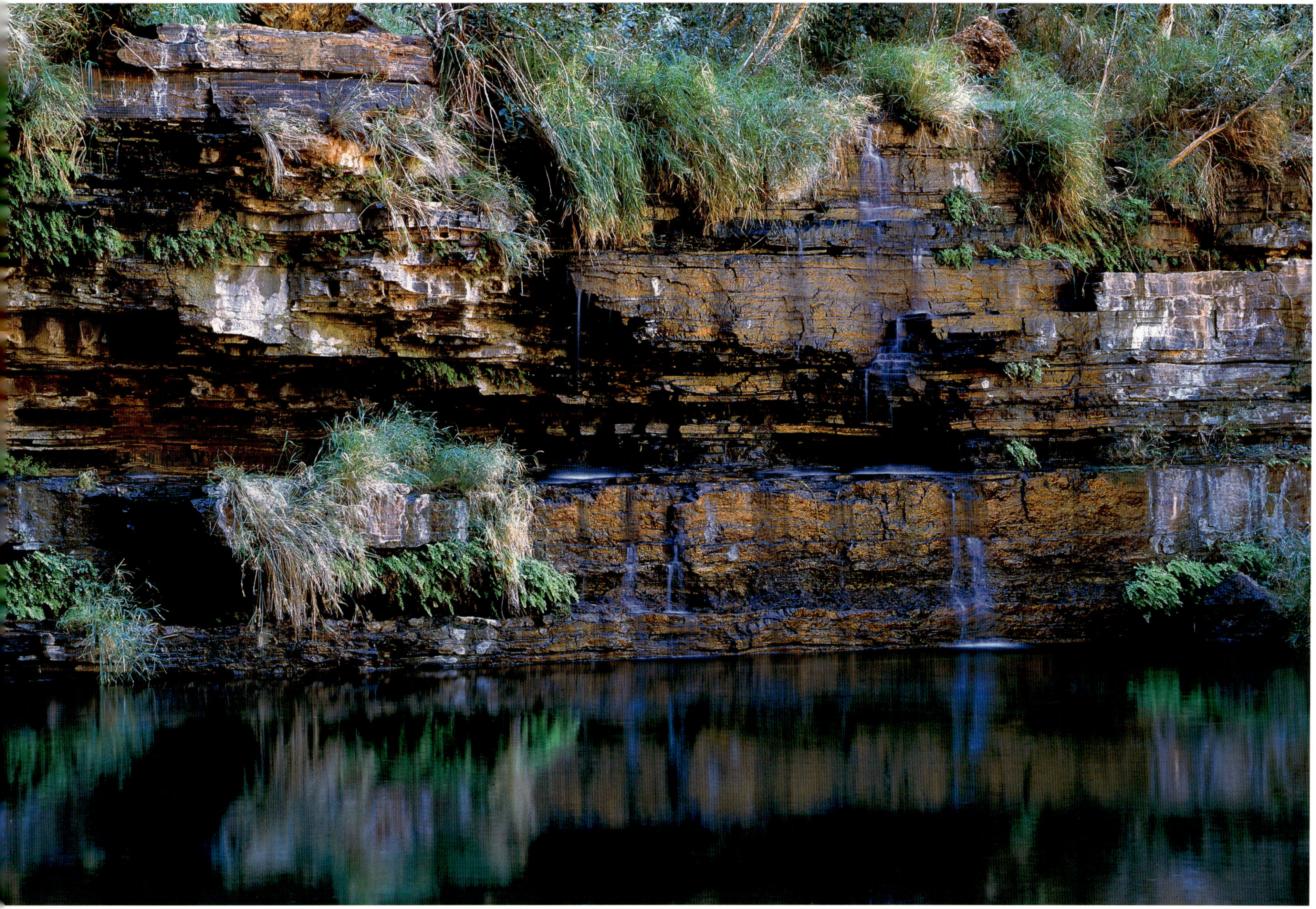

14 Hamersley Range from Mt Sheila Lookout, Pilbara

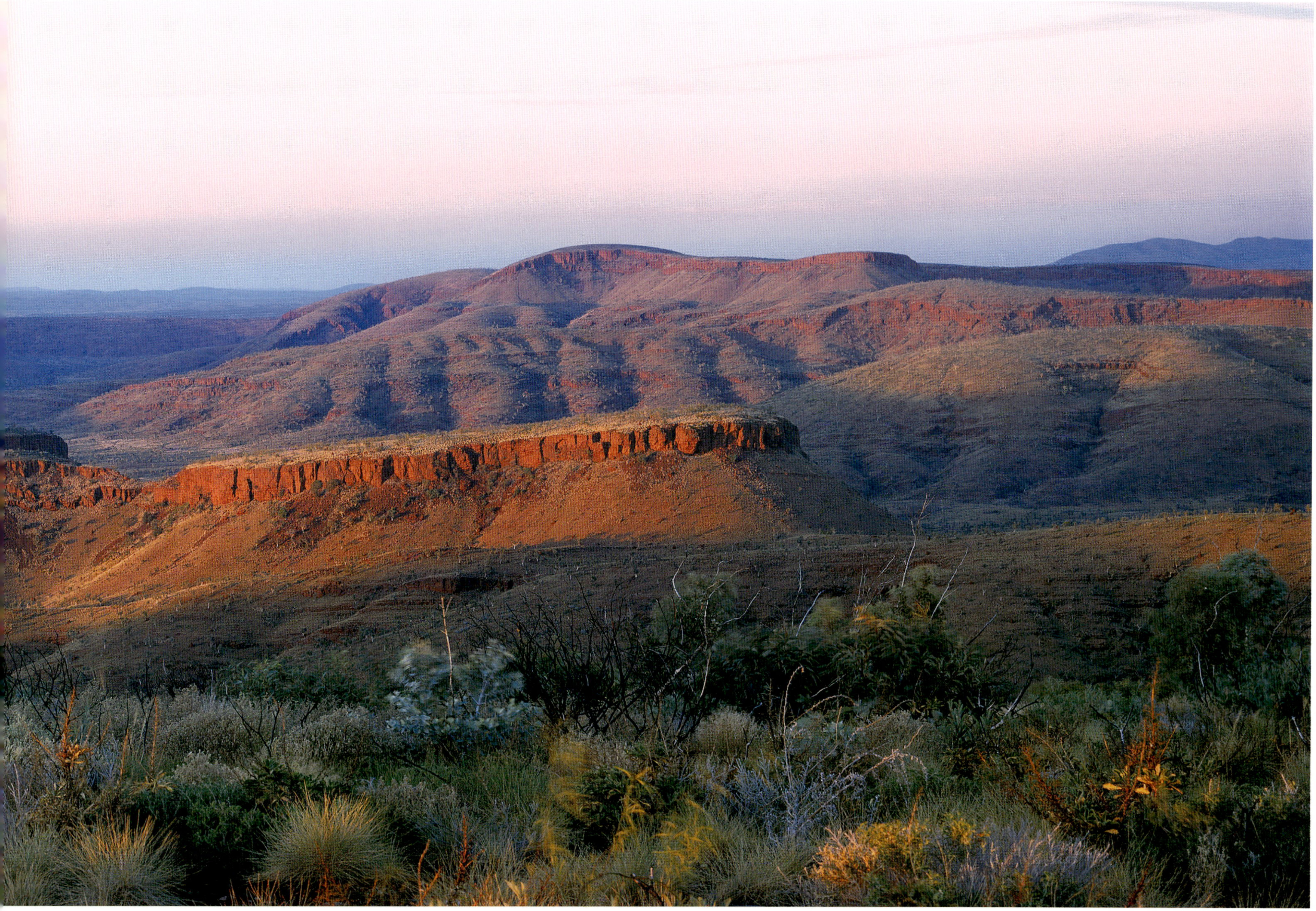

16 Hamersley Gorge, Karijini N.P.

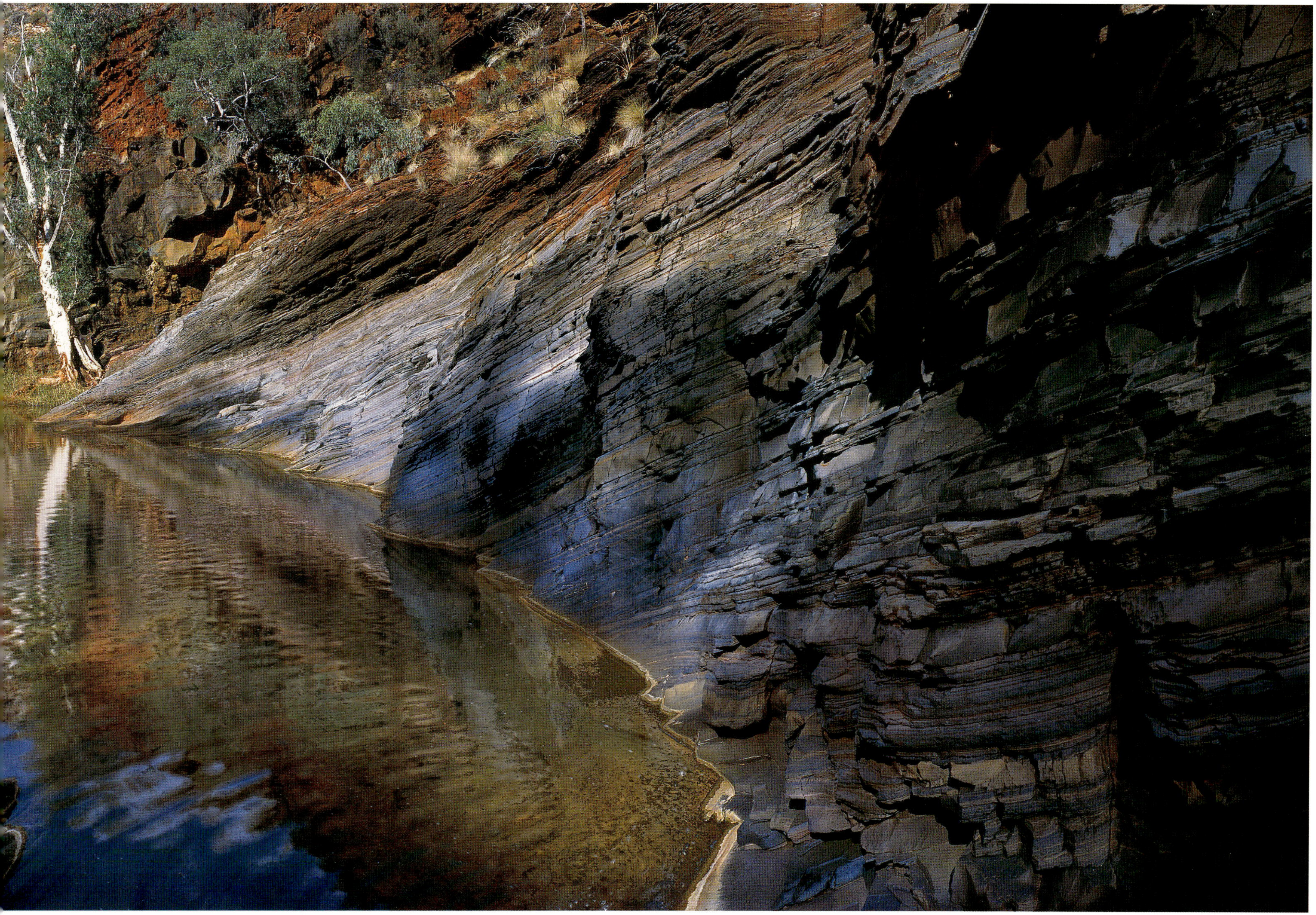

18 Hancock Gorge (after Kermit's Pool), Karijini N.P.

Hancock Gorge (towards end), Pilbara

20 Hamersley Gorge, Karijini N.P.

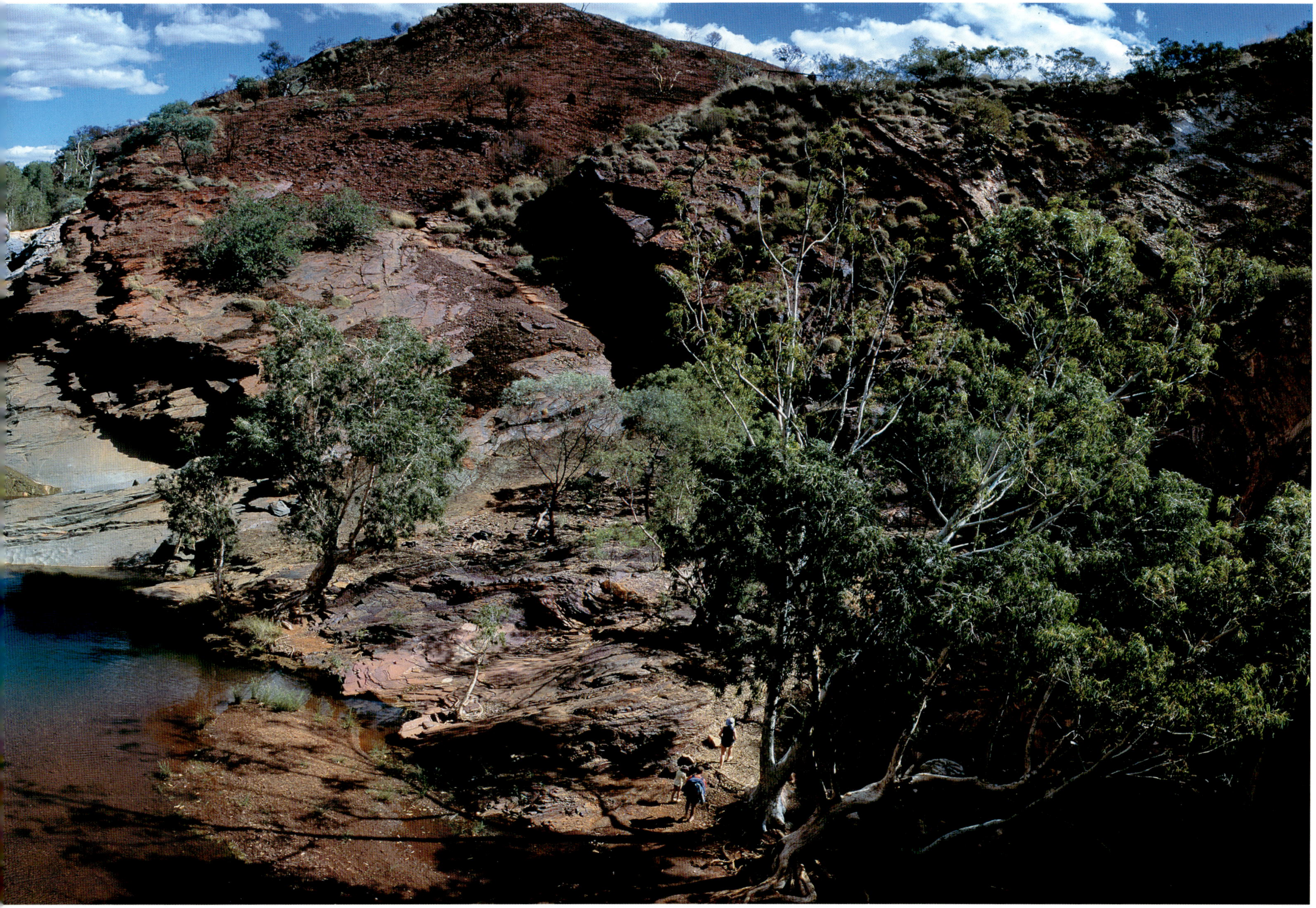

Handrail Pool, Weano Gorge, Karijini N.P.

23

Millstream Lookout, Millstream Chichester National Park, Pilbara

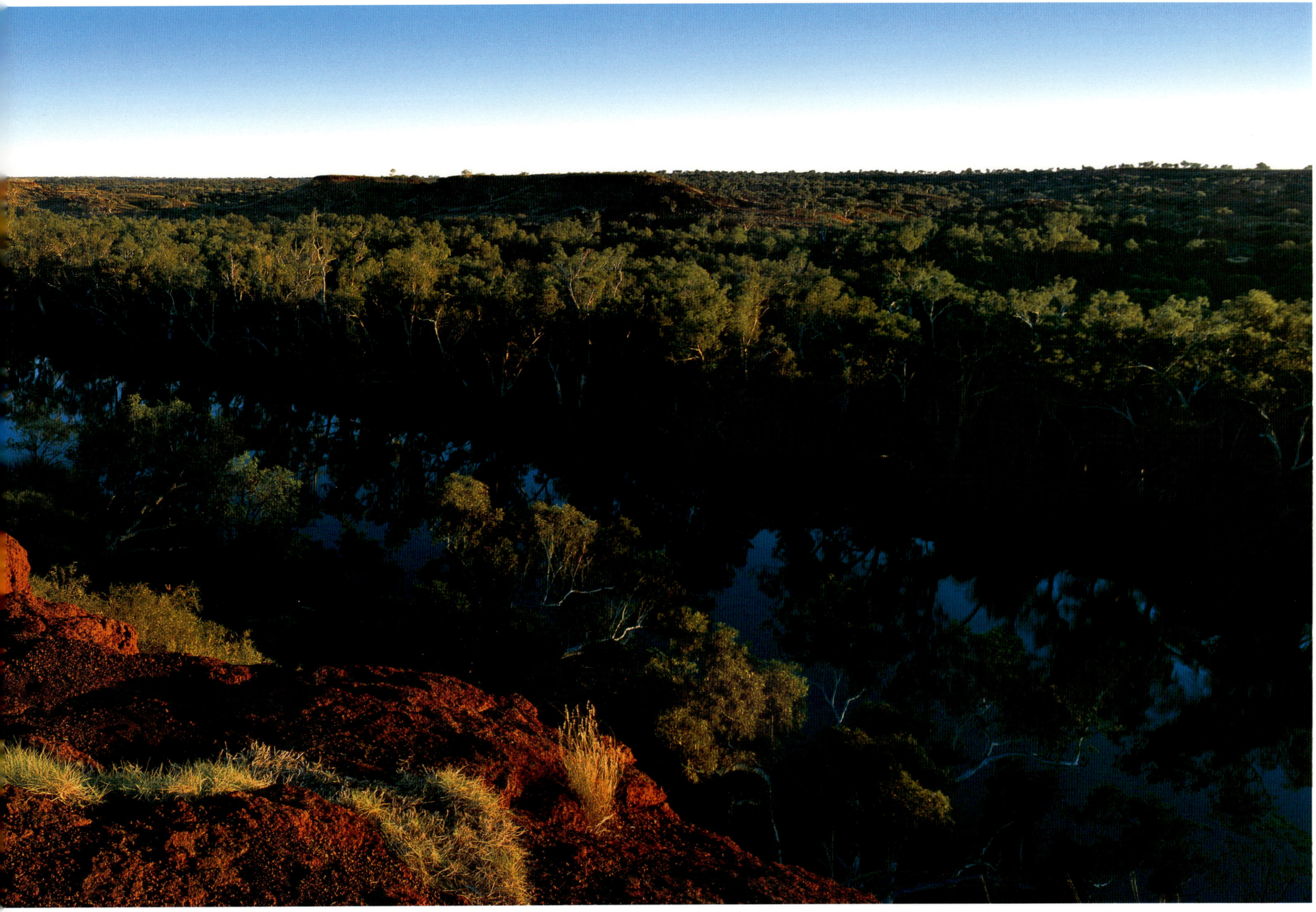

26   Hamersley Gorge, Karijini N.P.

27

32 Spa Pool, Hamersley Gorge, Karijini N.P.

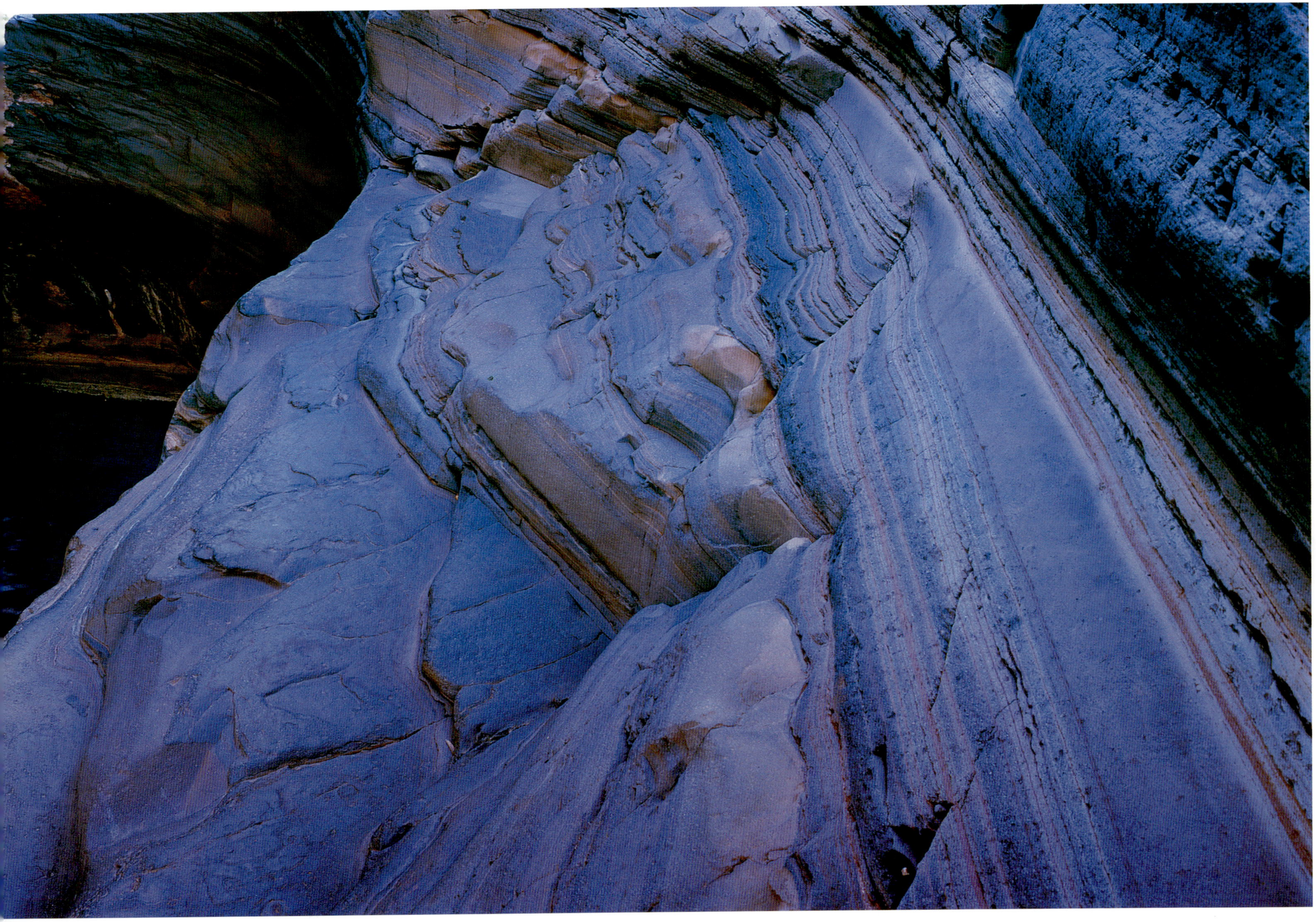

34 Last pool, Weano Gorge, Karijini N.P.

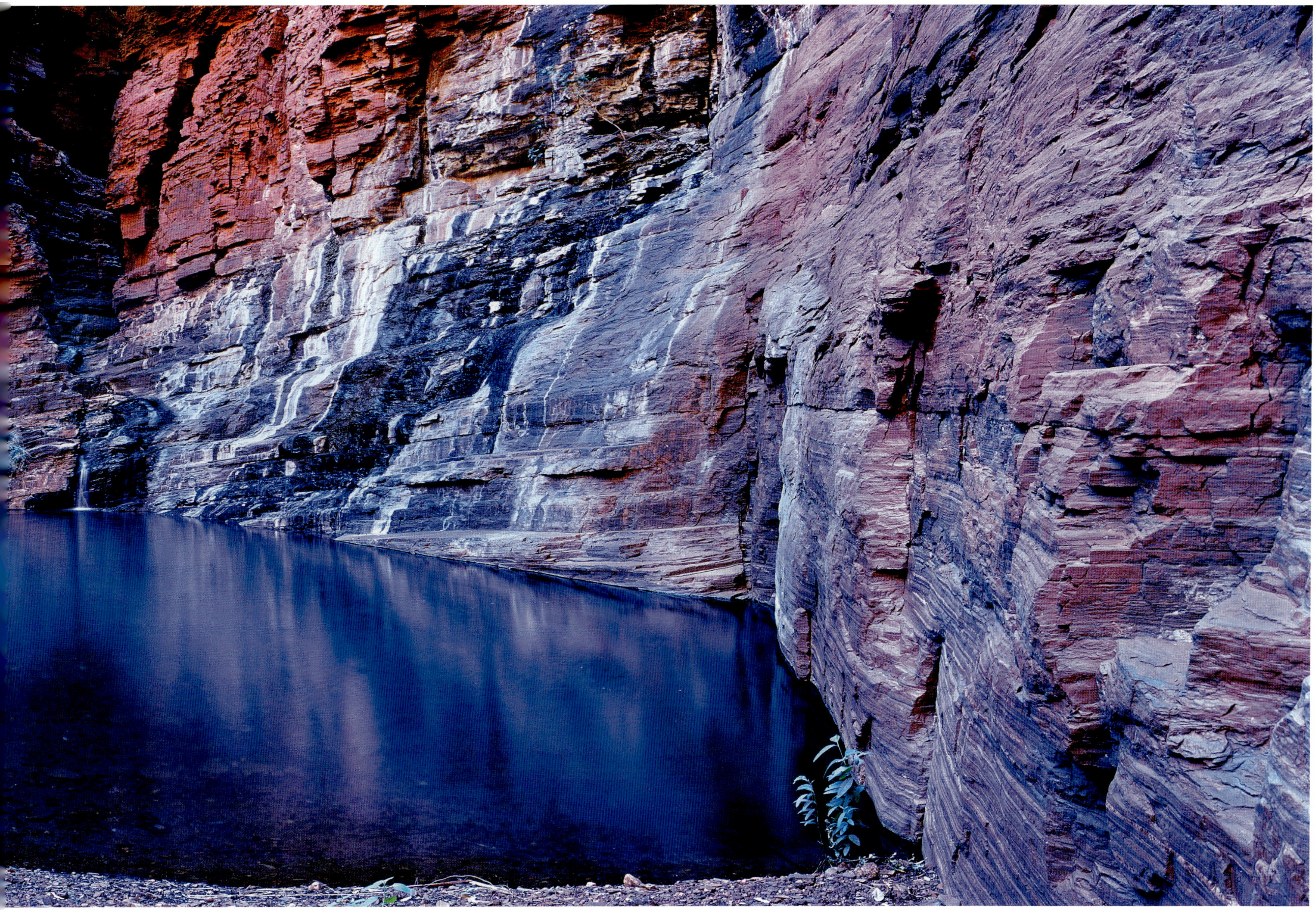

36 Weano Gorge, Karijini N.P.

Weano Gorge, Karijini N.P.

38 Fern Pool, Karijini N.P.

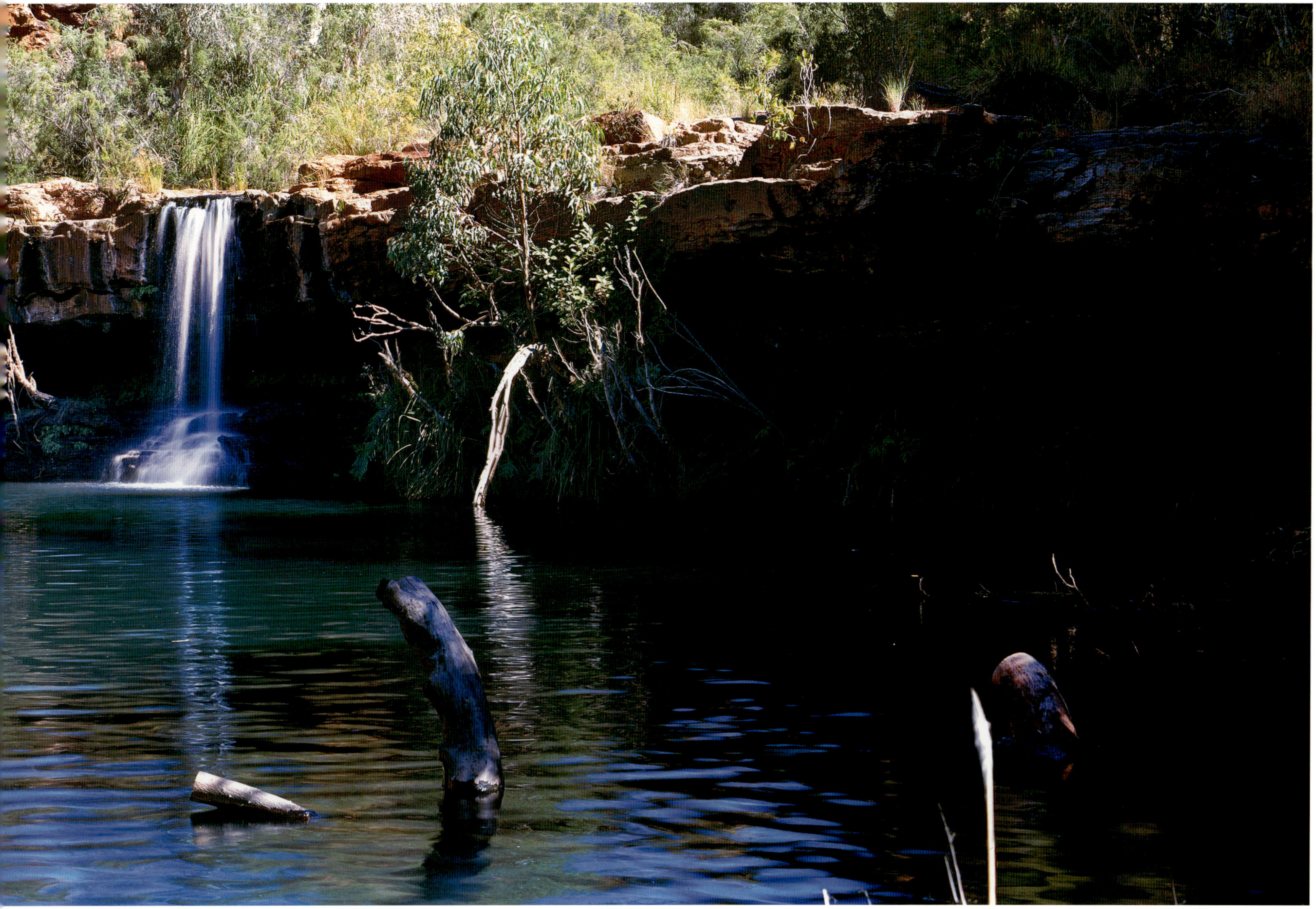

40   The historic town of Cossack founded 1863, Pilbara

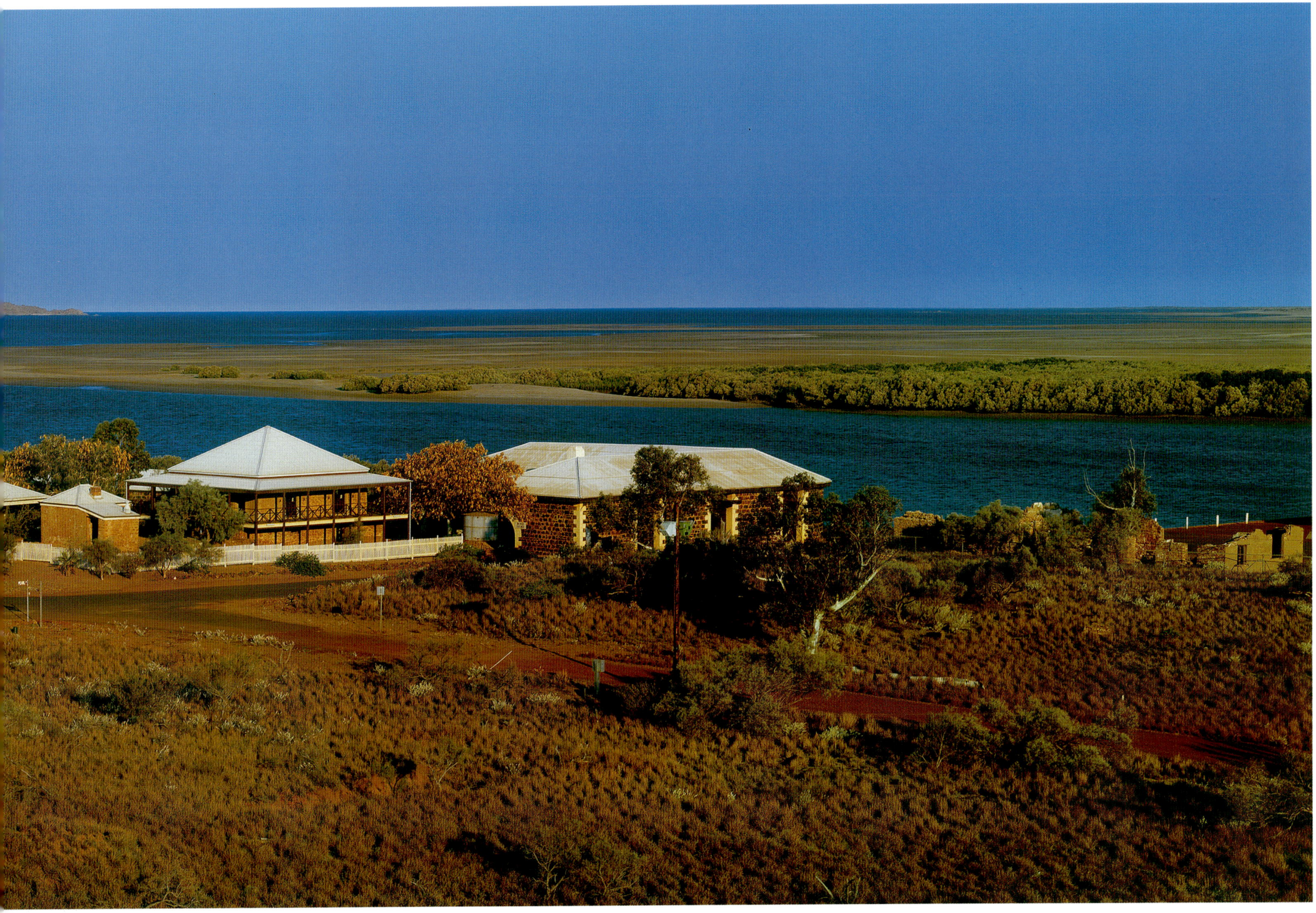

42 Cape Leveque, West Kimberley

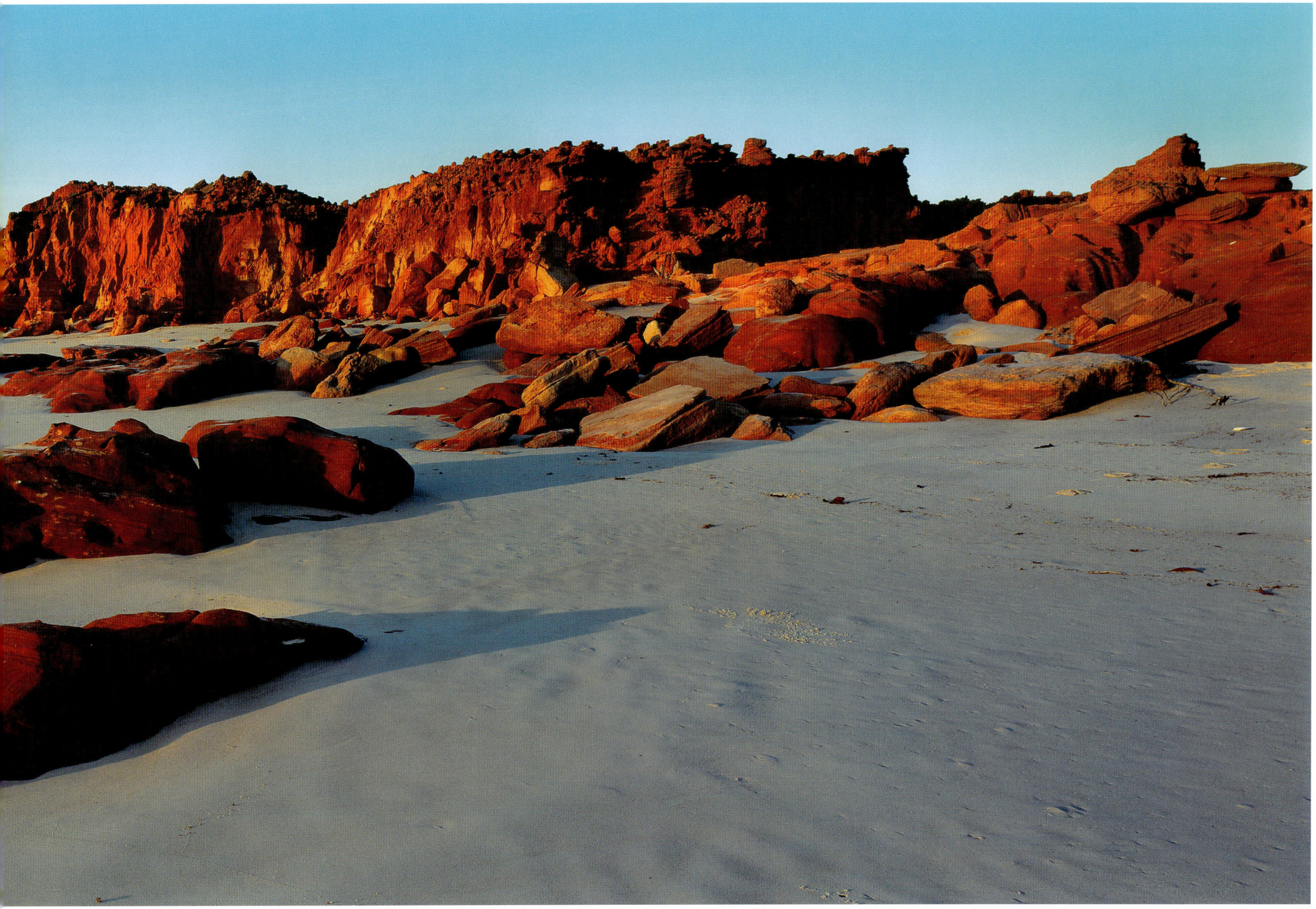

44 Cable Beach, Broome, Kimberley

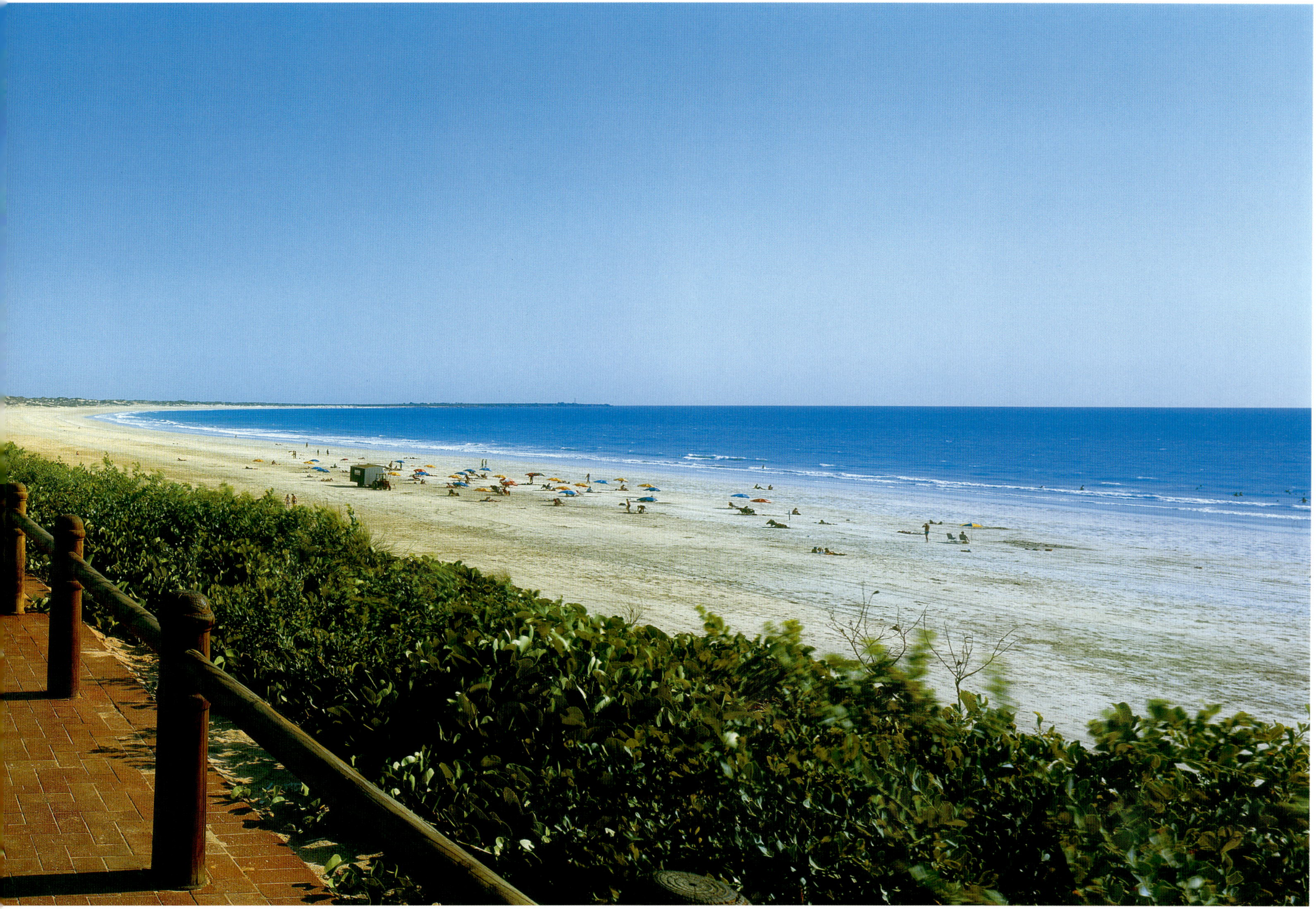

46 Distant pindan dunes, Cape Leveque, Kimberley

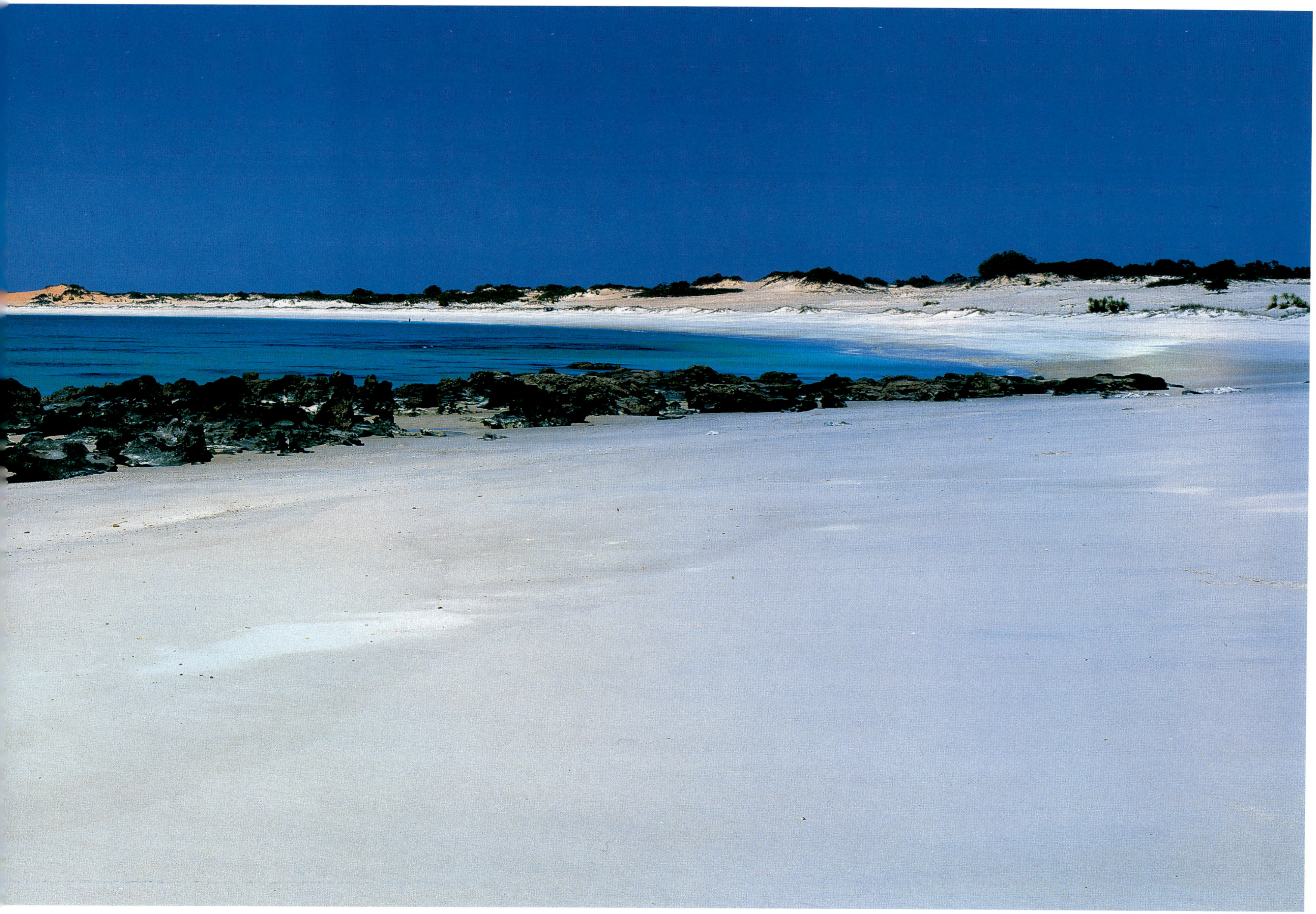

48 Red cliffs, Cape Leveque, West Kimberley

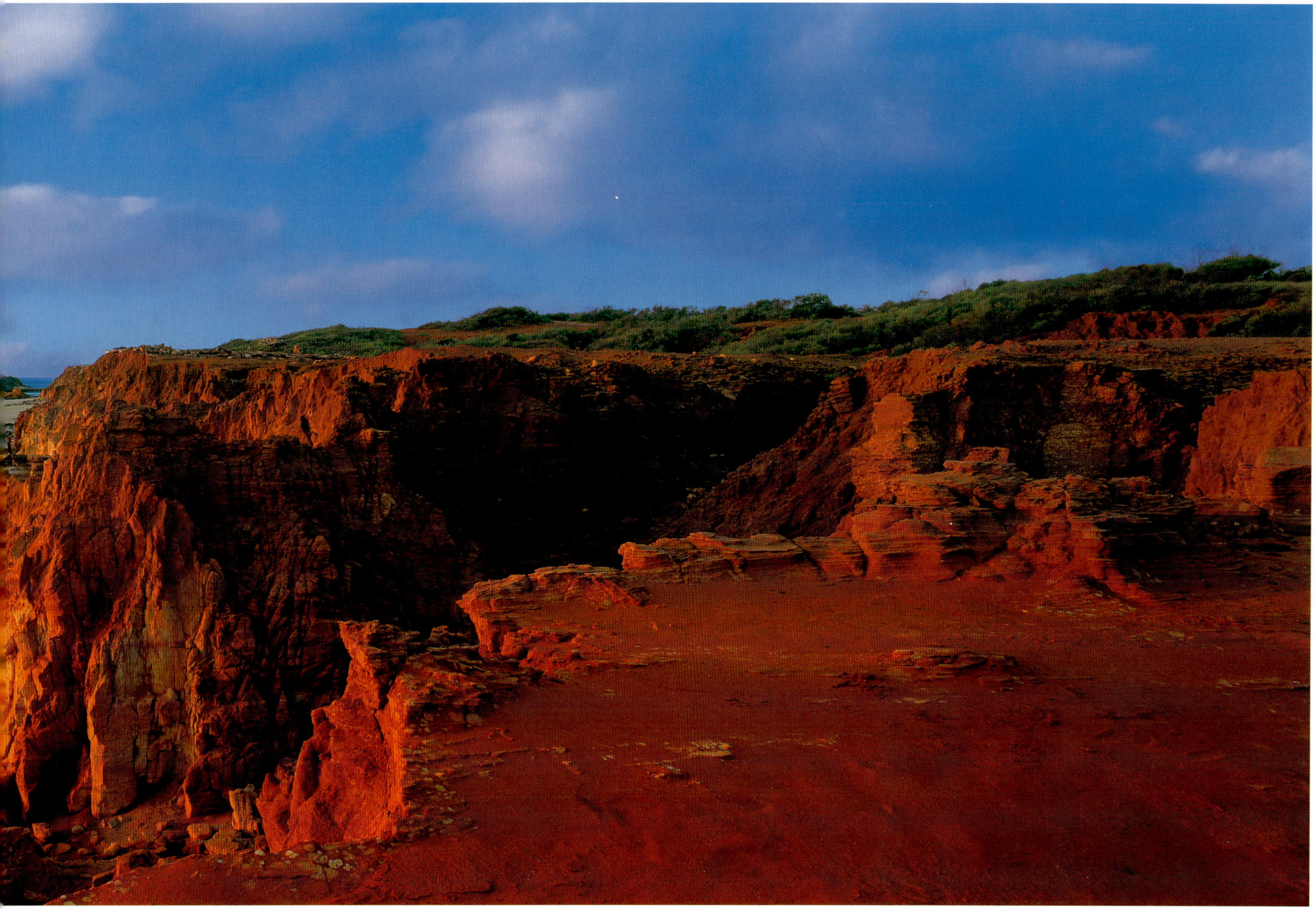

50   Ganthium Point sunset, Broome, Kimberley

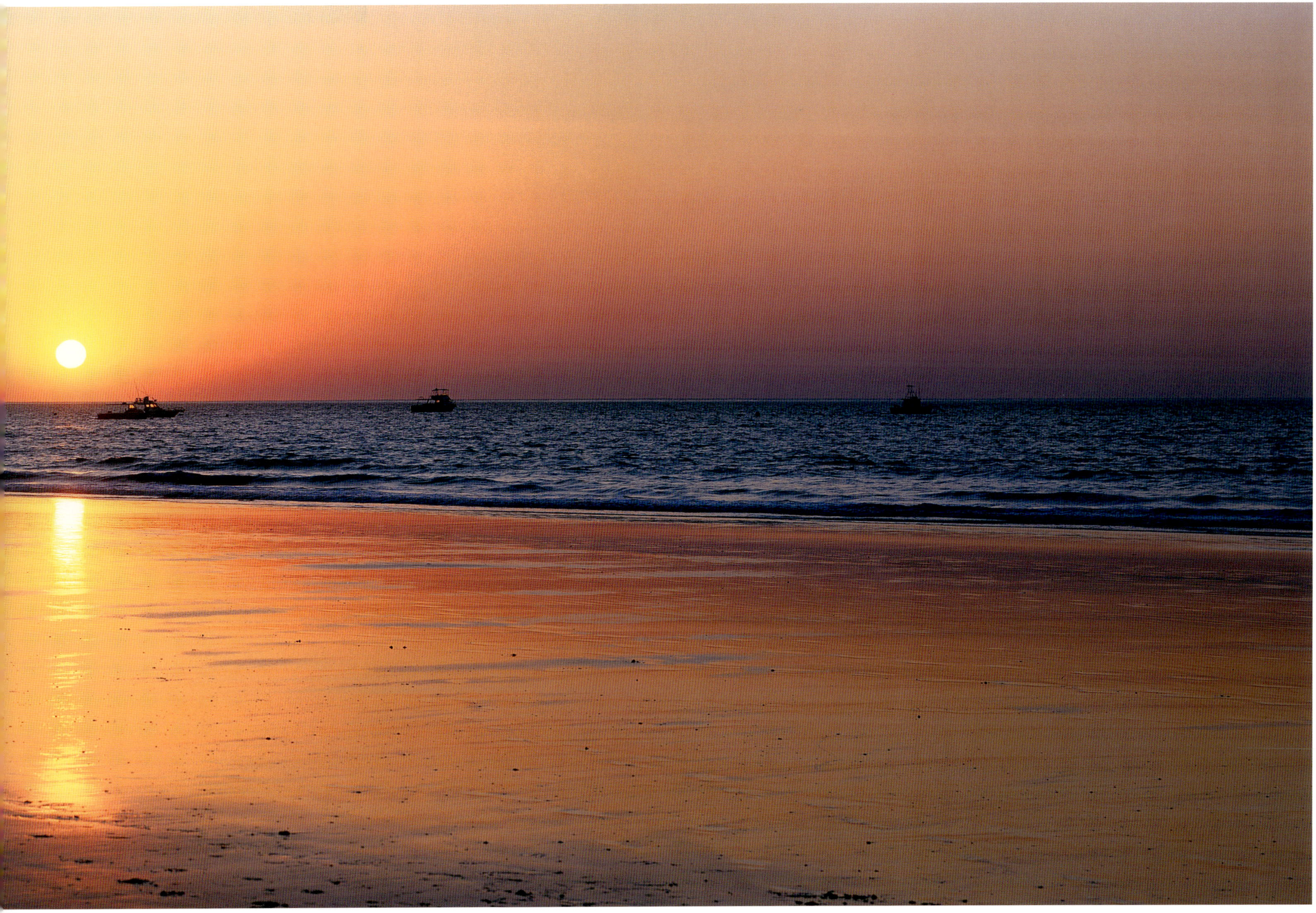

52 Cable Beach camels, Broome, Kimberley

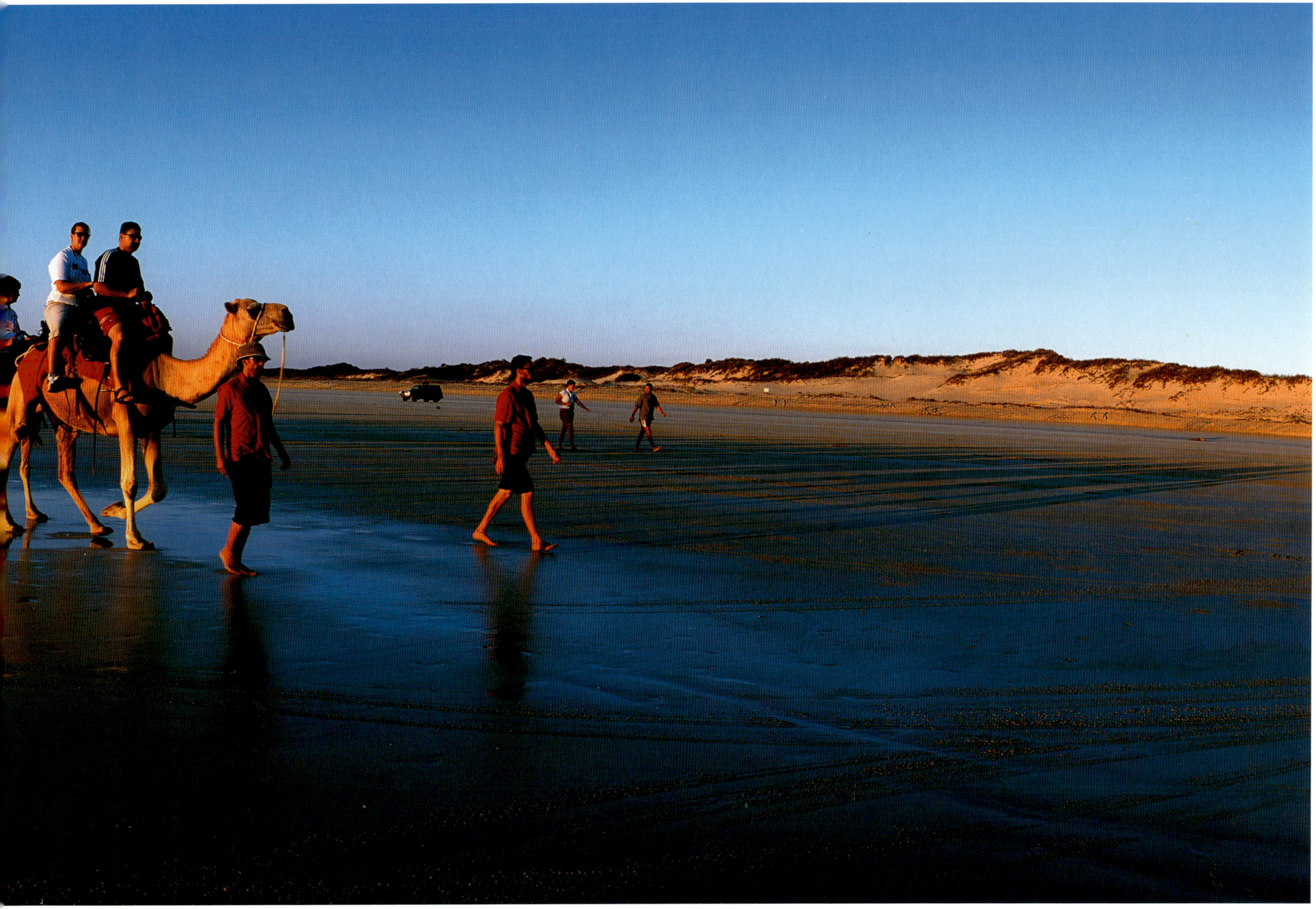

54 'Spirit of Broome' hovercraft base, Roebuck Bay, Broome, Kimberley

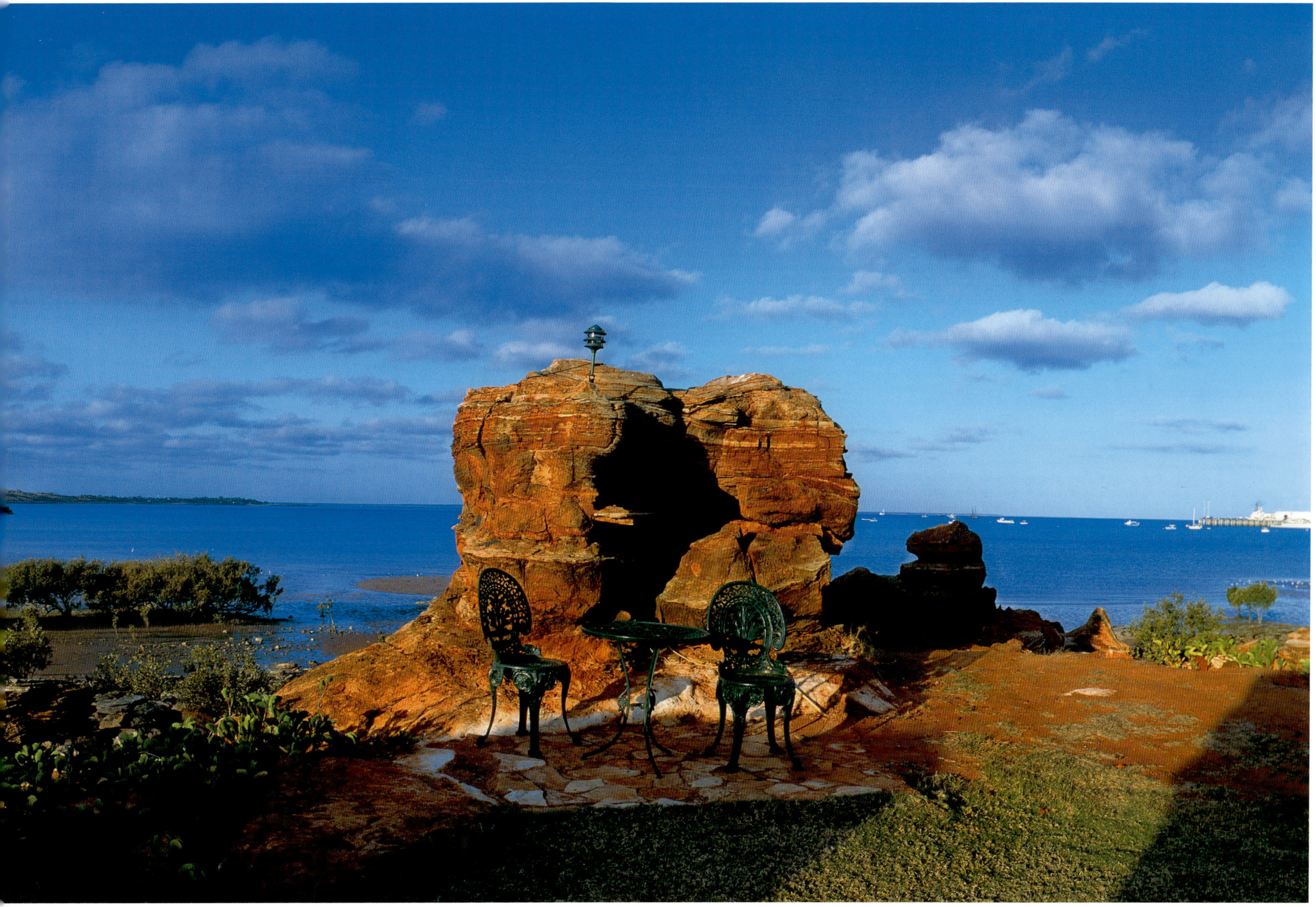

56 Sunrise at Cape Leveque, Kimberley

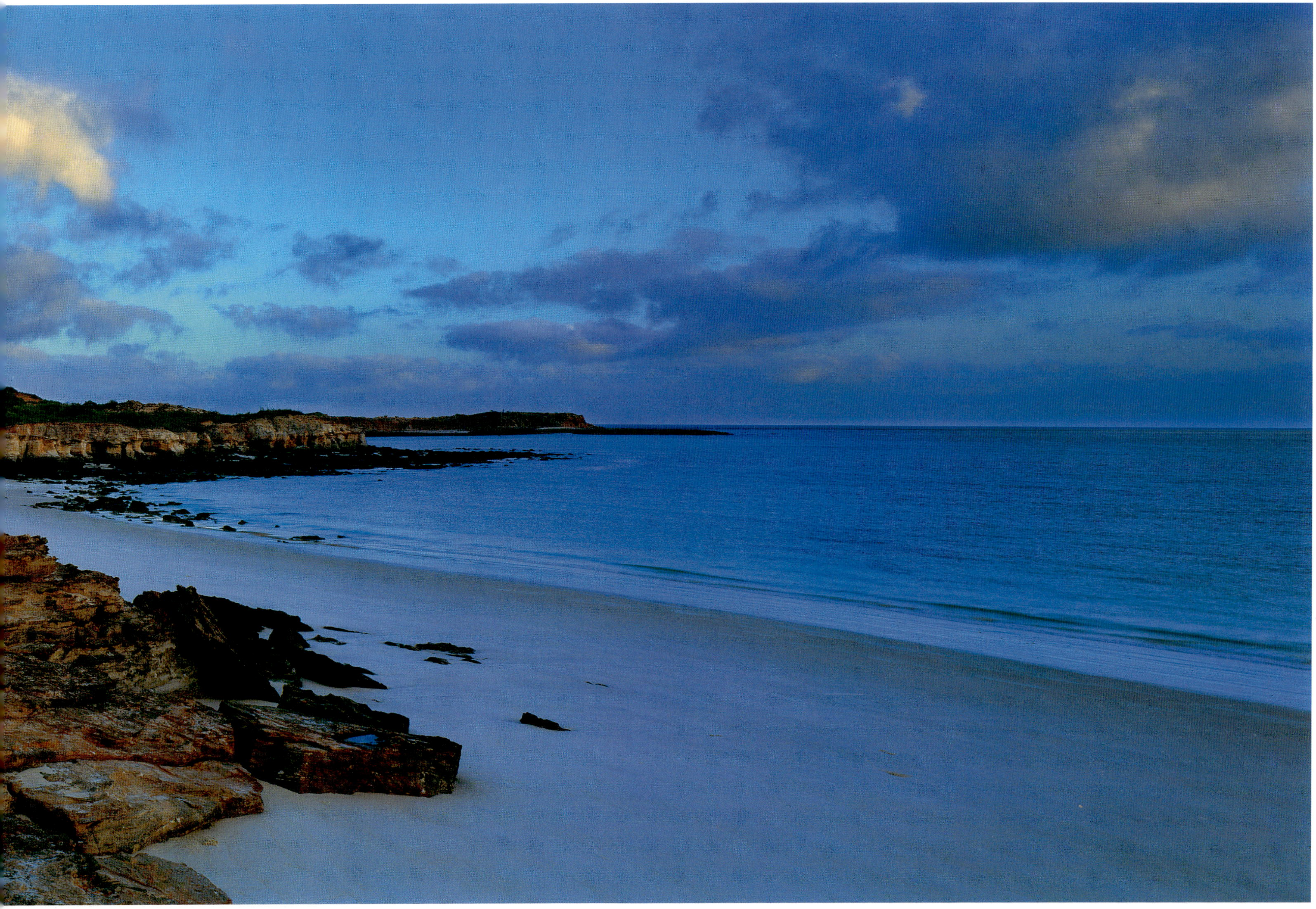

58 Cape Leveque, West Kimberley

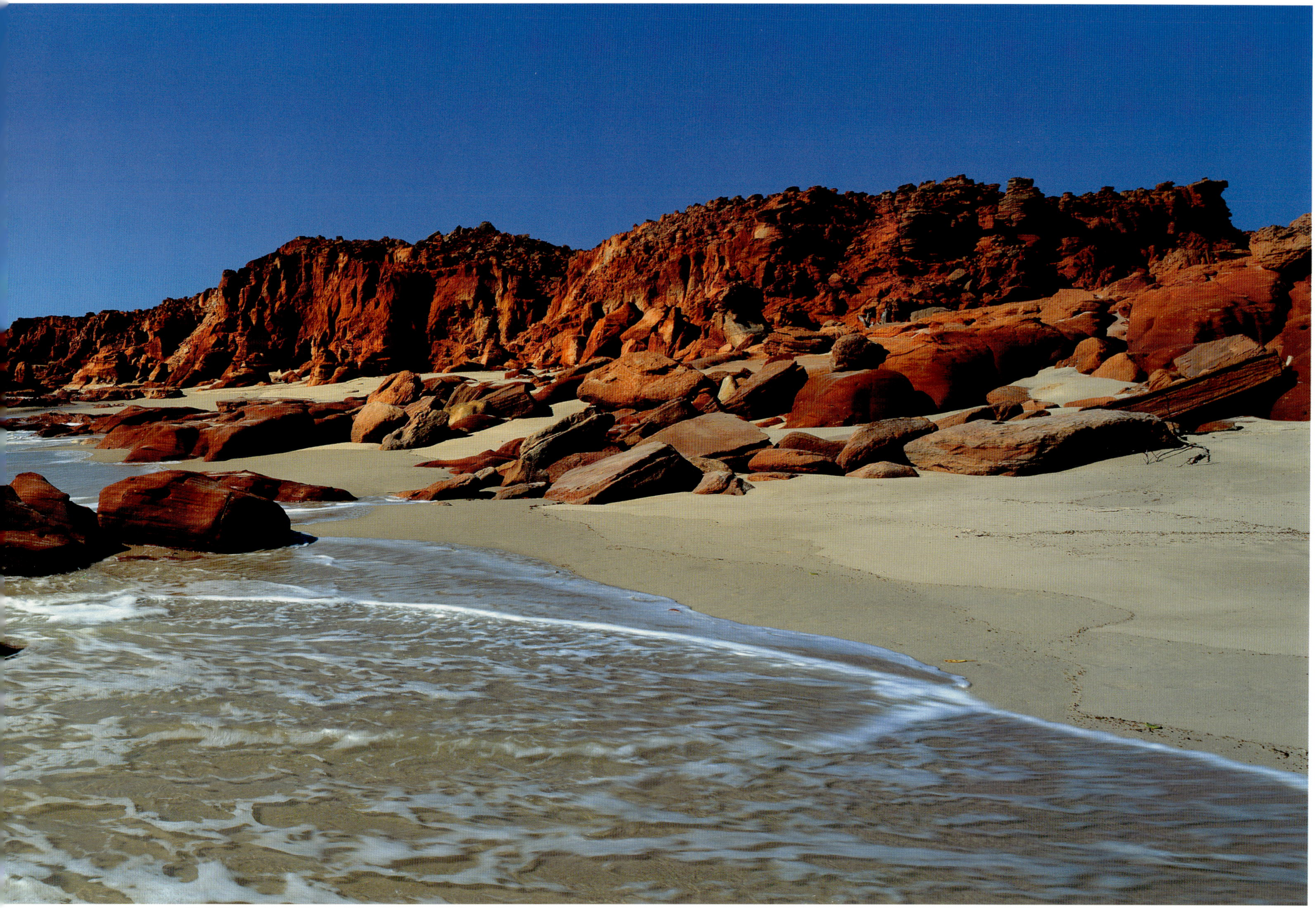

Beehive Domes, Bungle Bungles, Kimberley

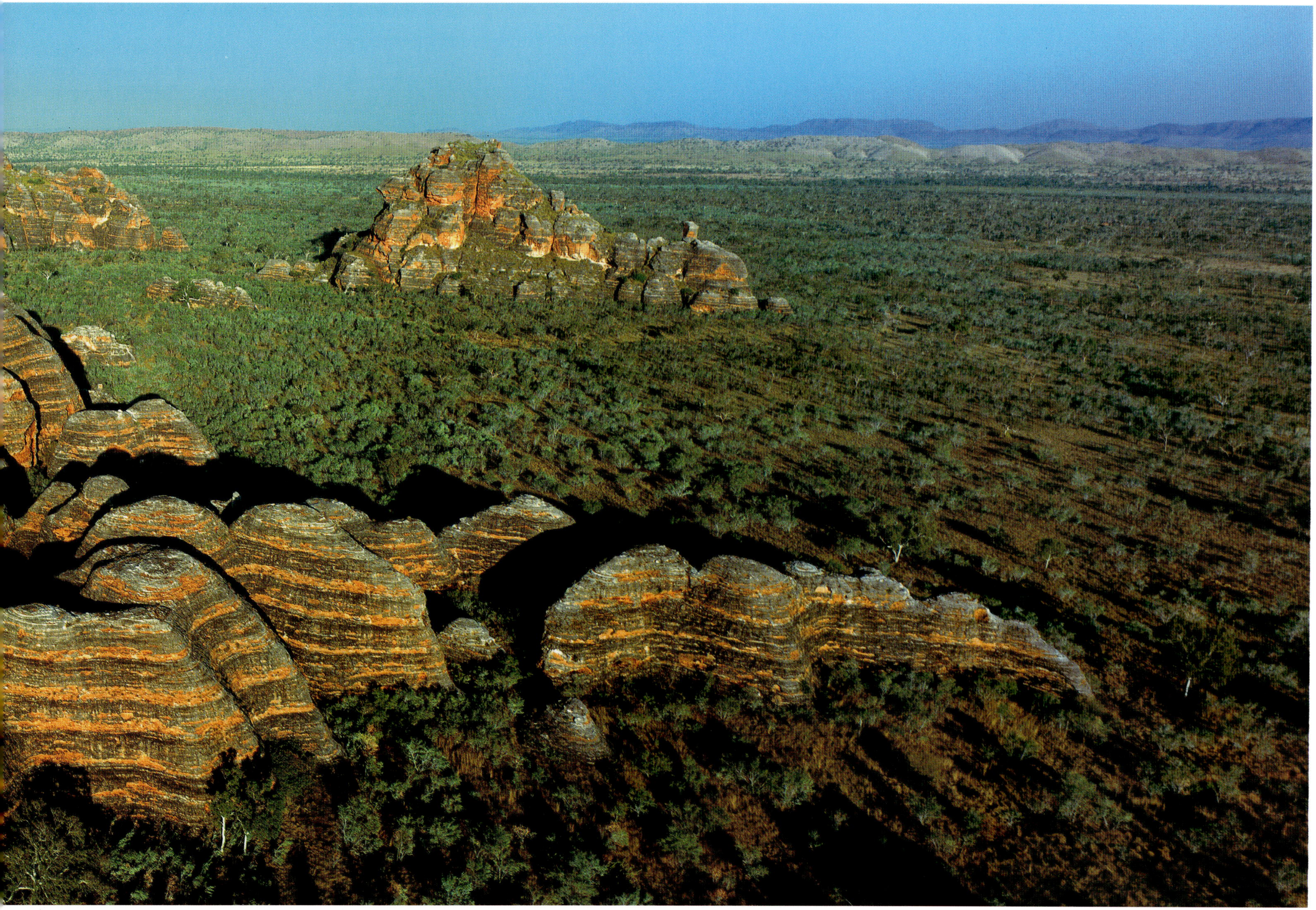

Bird's eye view, Bungle Bungles, Kimberley

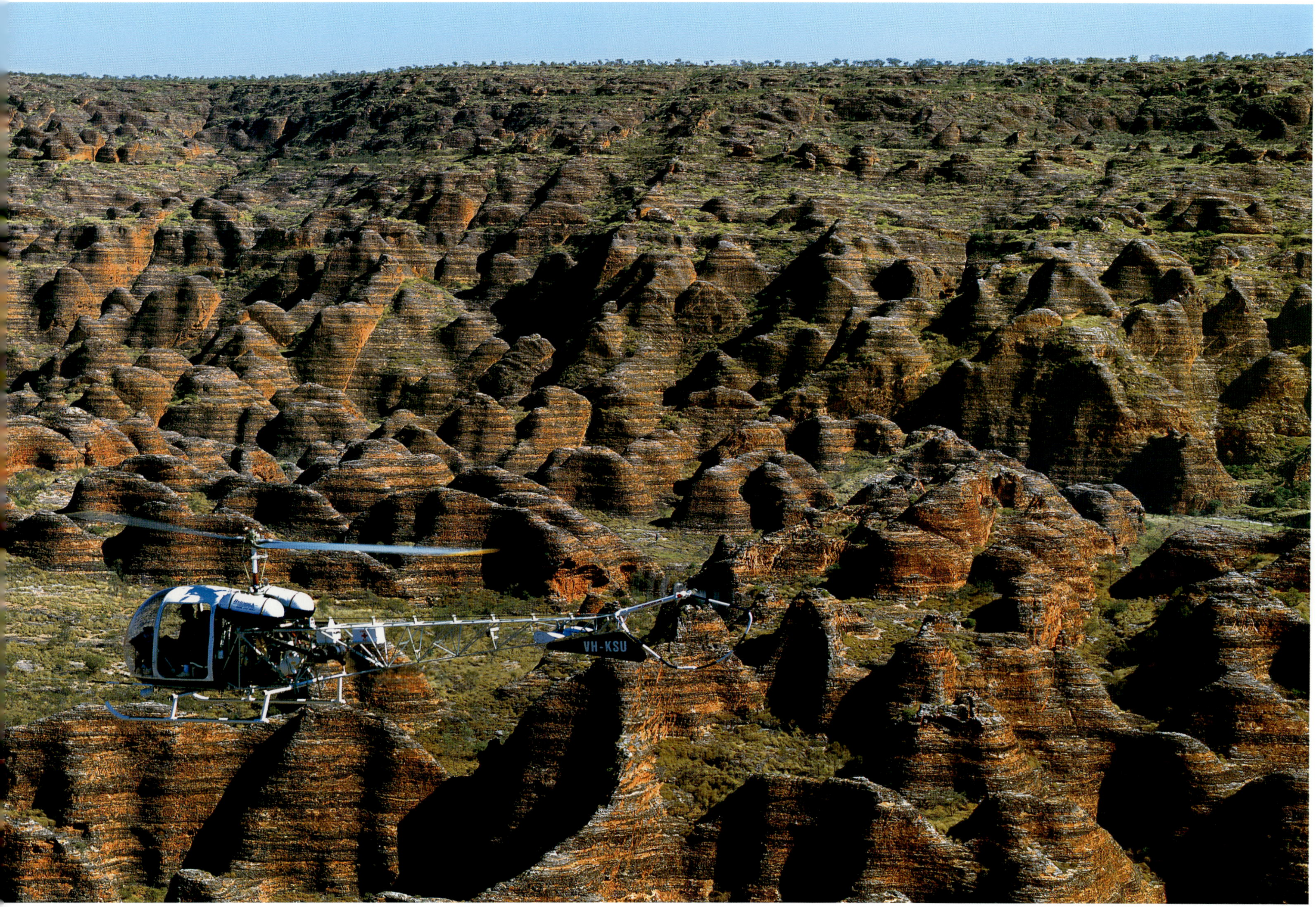
VH-KSU

64   Distant Domes, Bungle Bungles, Kimberley

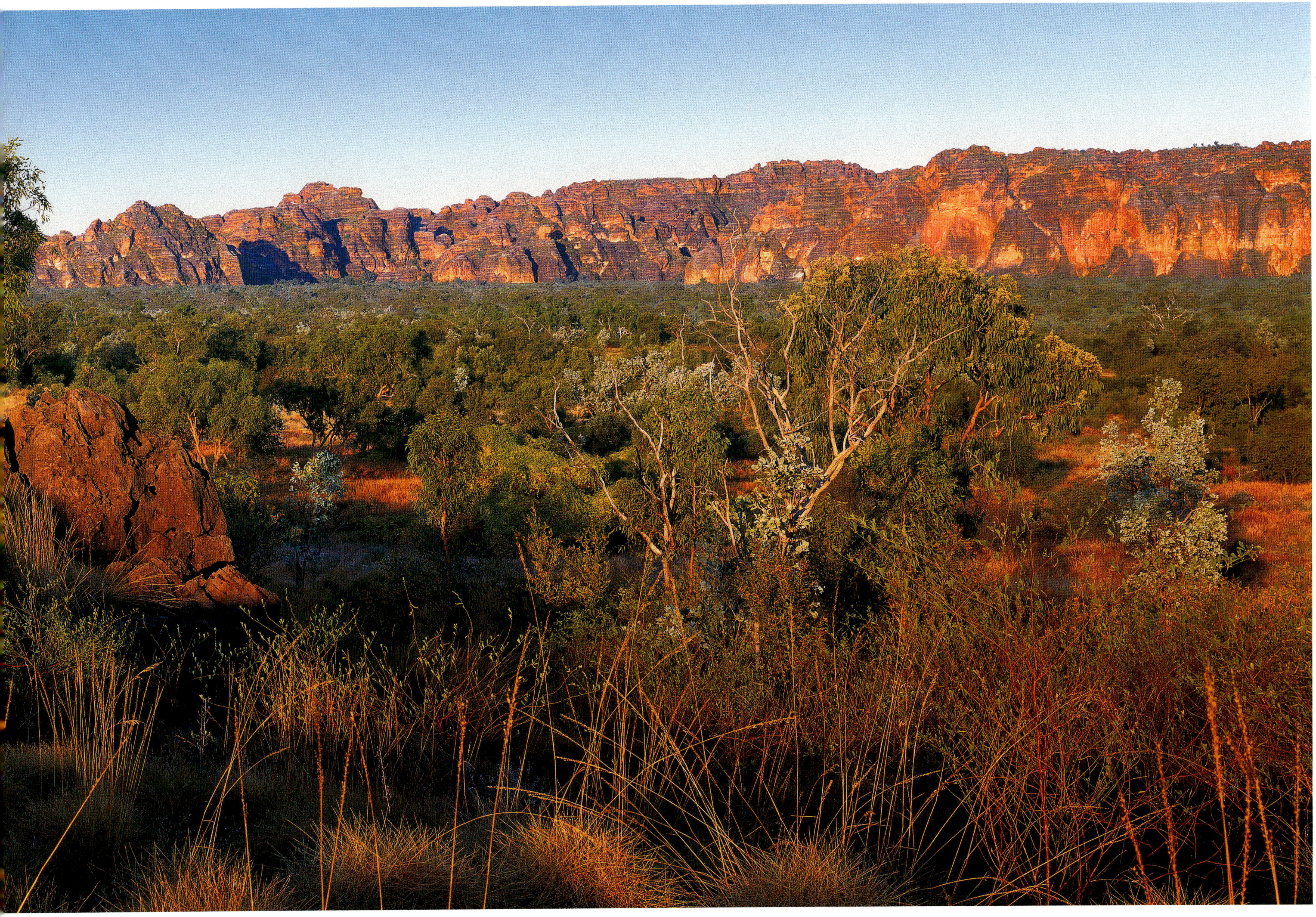

66   Western wall, Bungle Bungles, Kimberley

67

68　Walanginjdji Lookout, Bungle Bungles, Kimberley

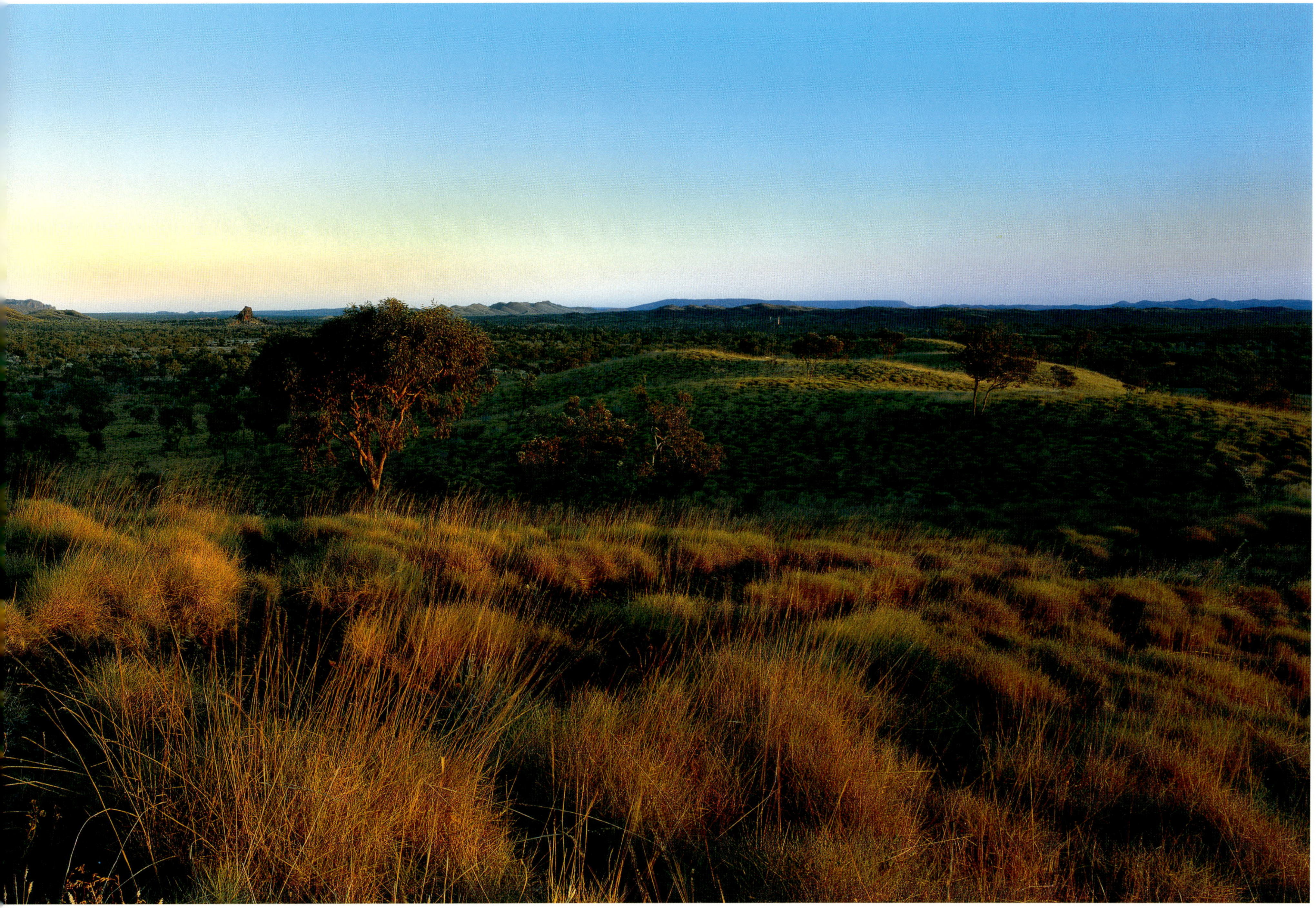

70   Echidna Chasm entrance, Bungle Bungles, Kimberley

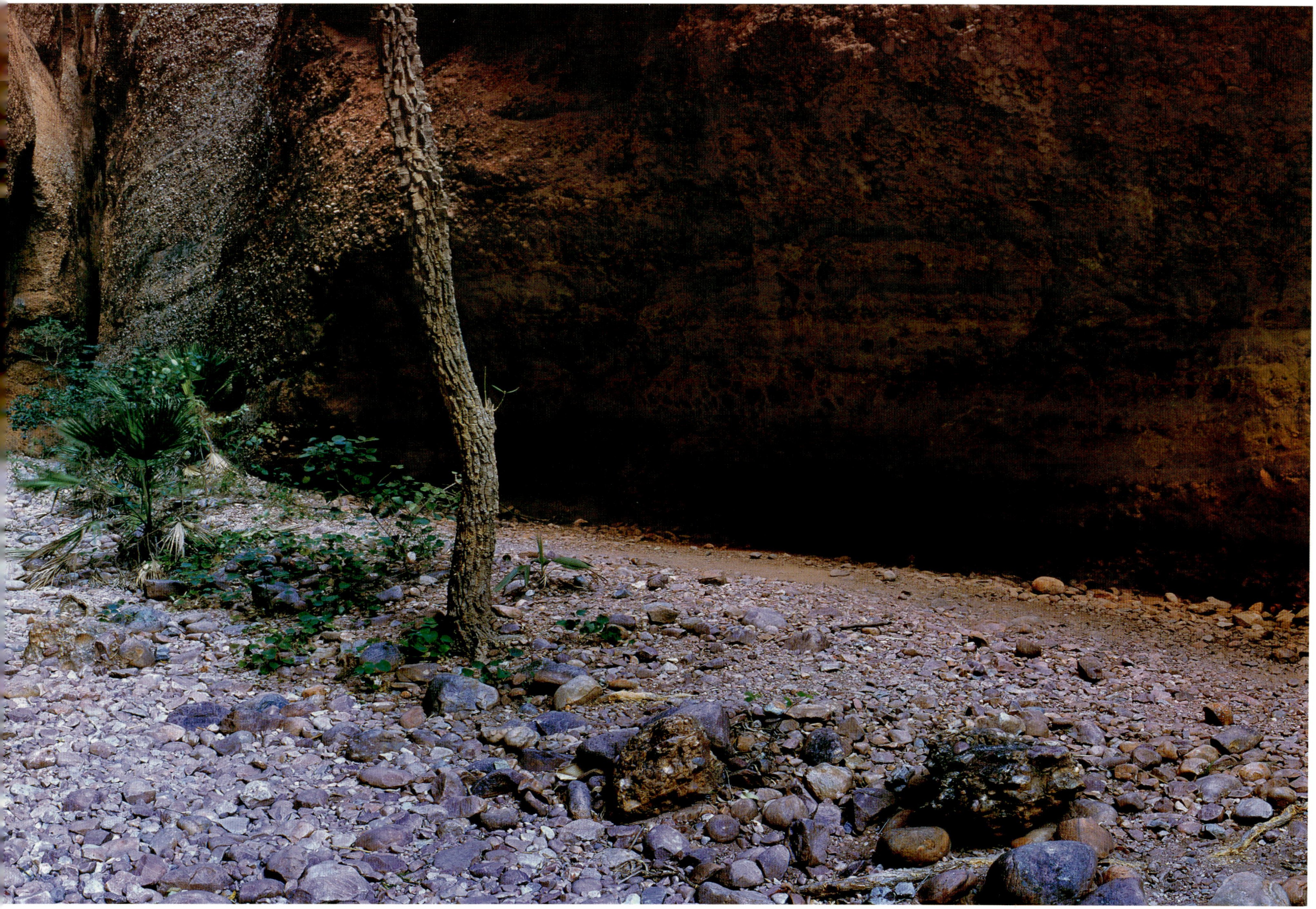

72 Froghole Gorge, Bungle Bungles, Kimberley

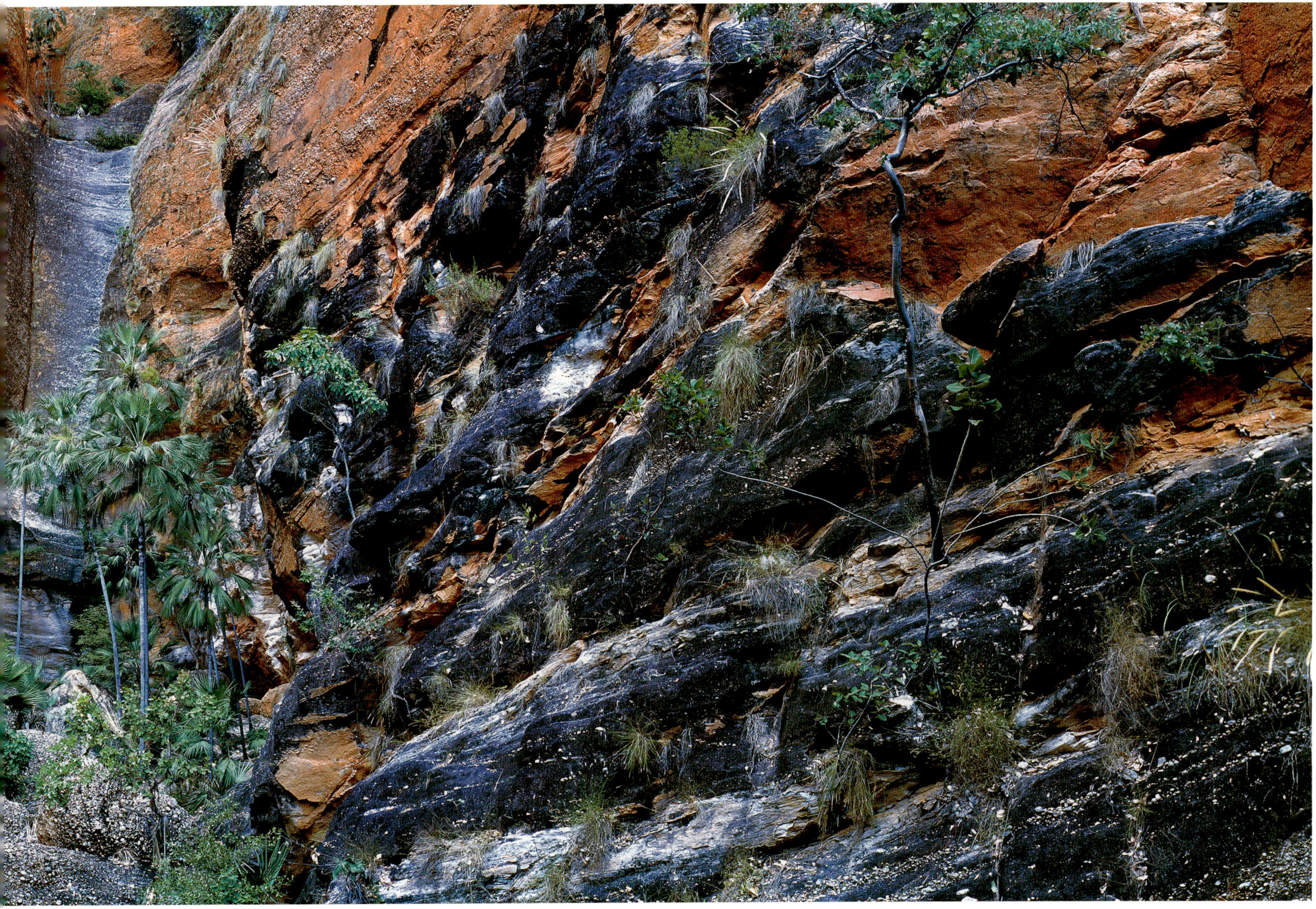

74 Bungle Bungles, Kimberley

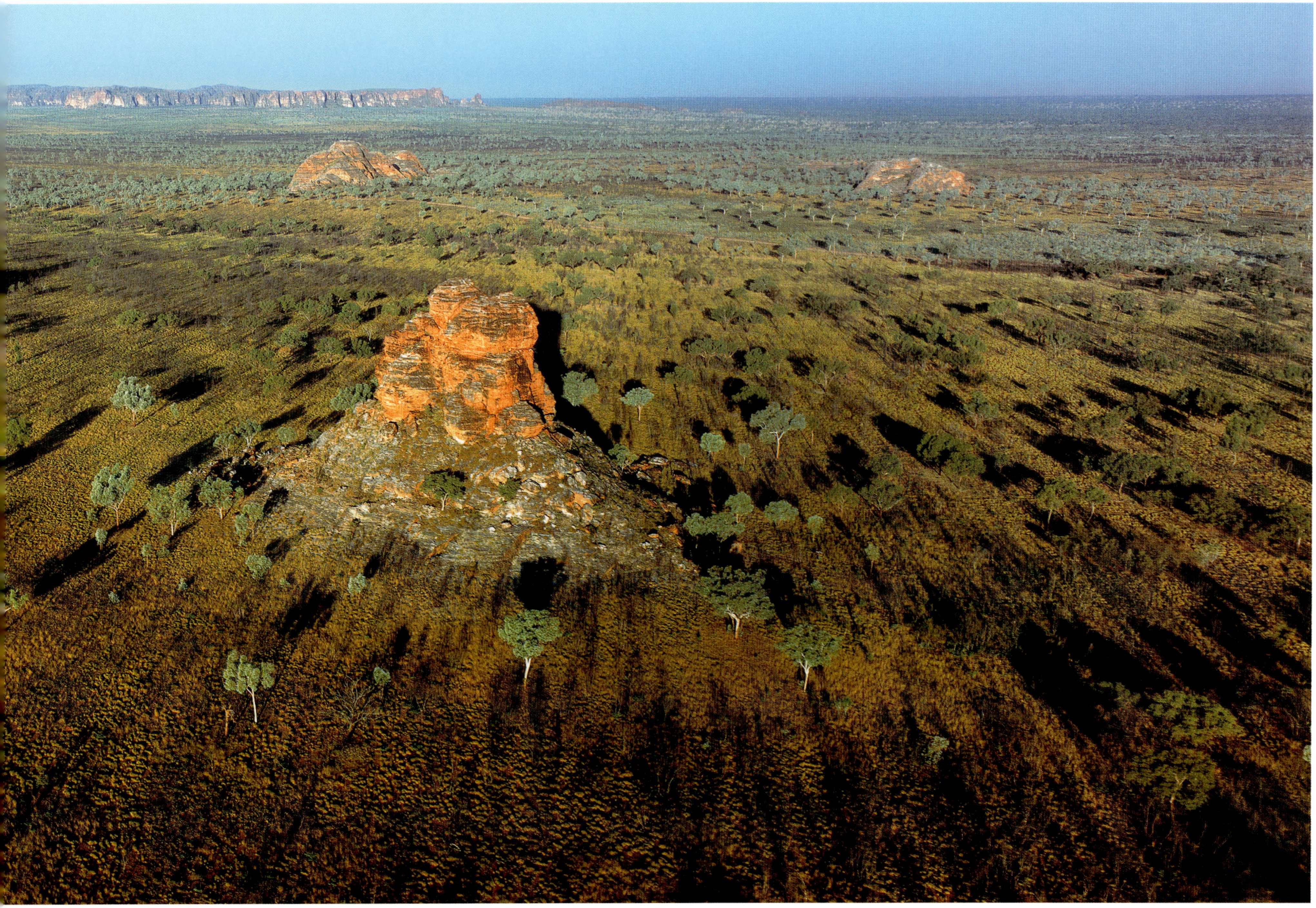

76 Bungle Bungles, Kimberley

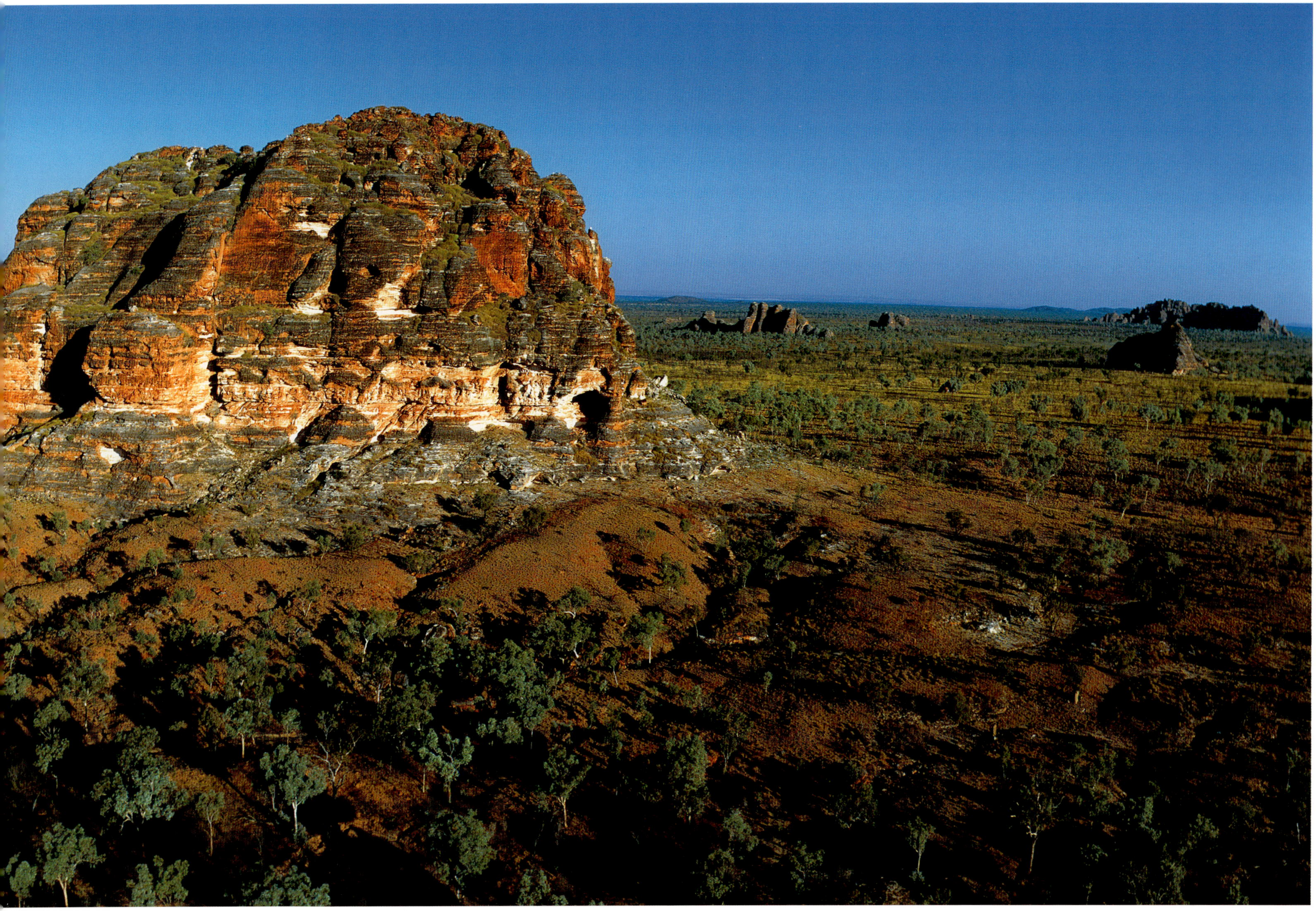

78 Cathedral Gorge Amphitheatre, Bungle Bungles, Kimberley

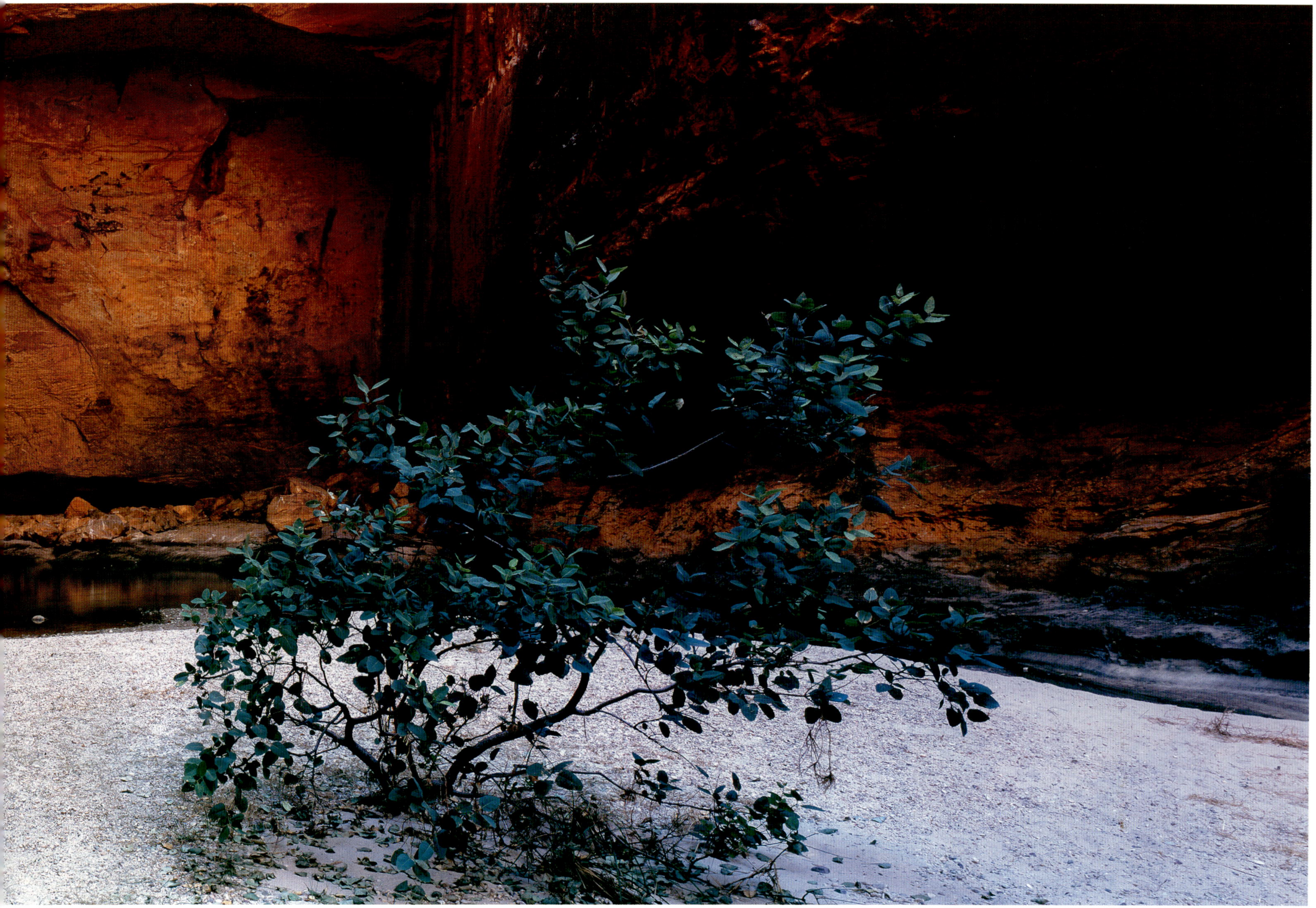

80 Natural sandstone chimney, Bungle Bungles, Kimberley

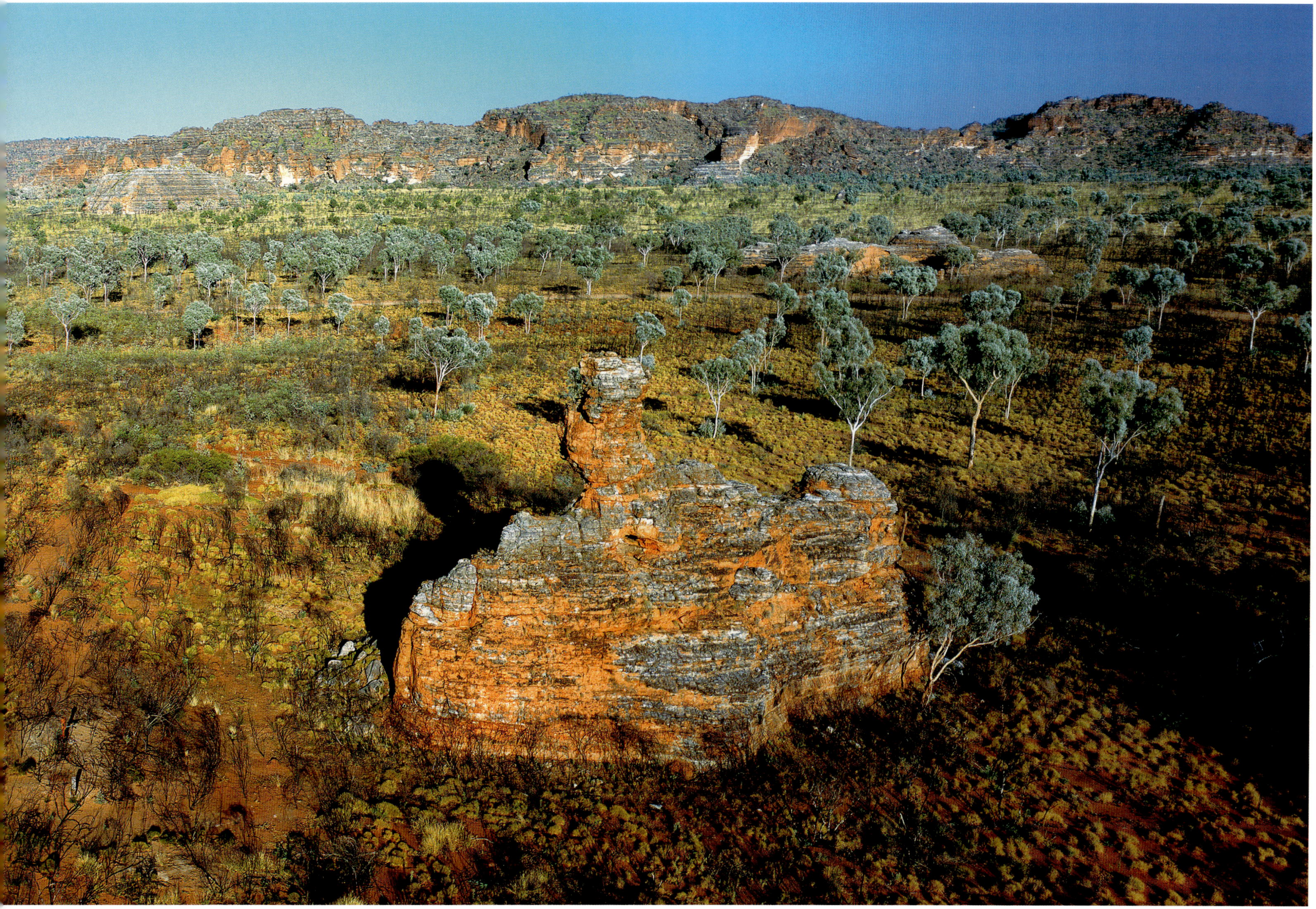

Beehive Domes and Piccaninny Creek, Bungle Bungles, Kimberley

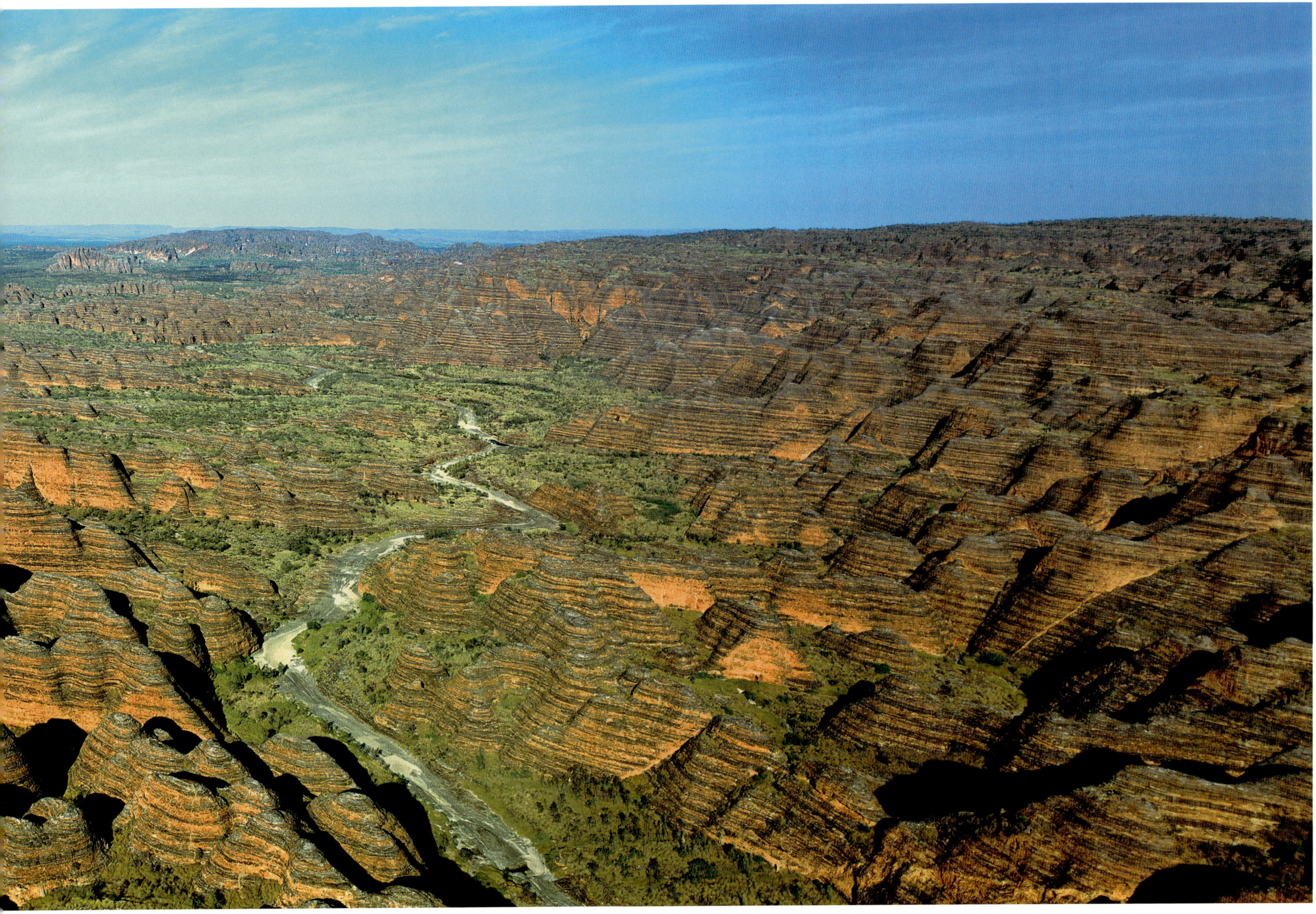

84 Scattered domes, Bungle Bungles, Kimberley

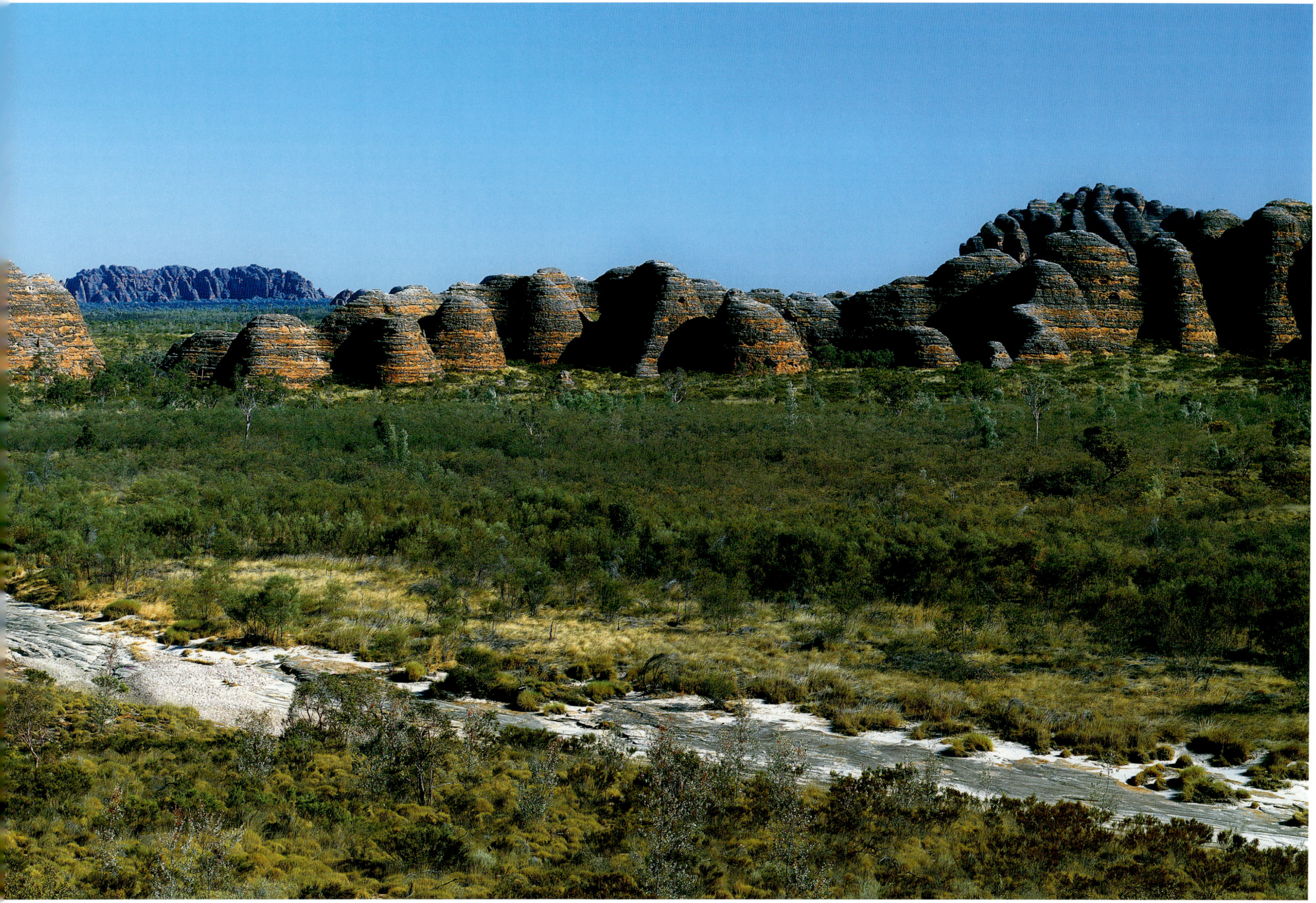

Beehive Domes, Bungle Bungles, Kimberley

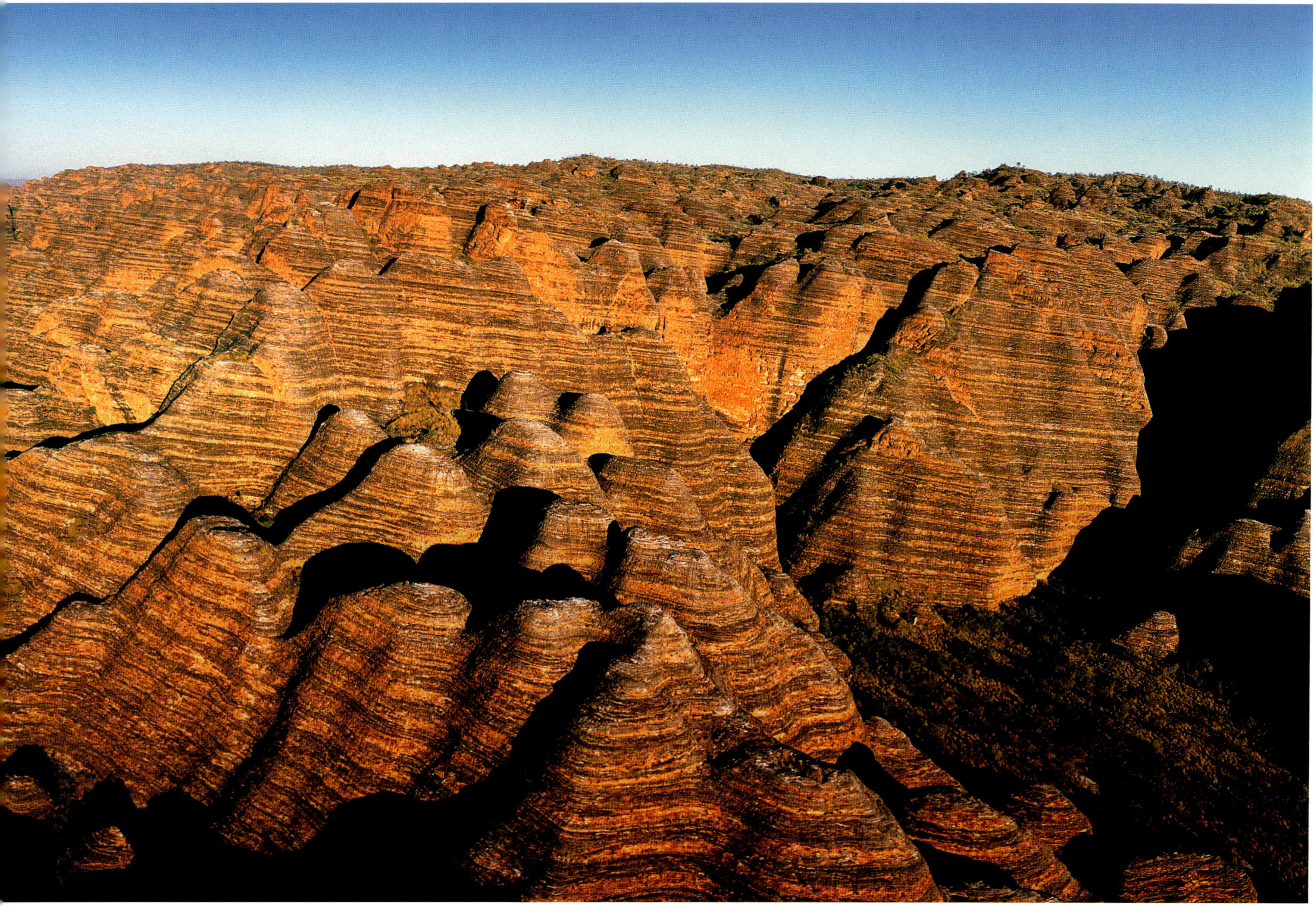

88 Lake Argyle, West Kimberley

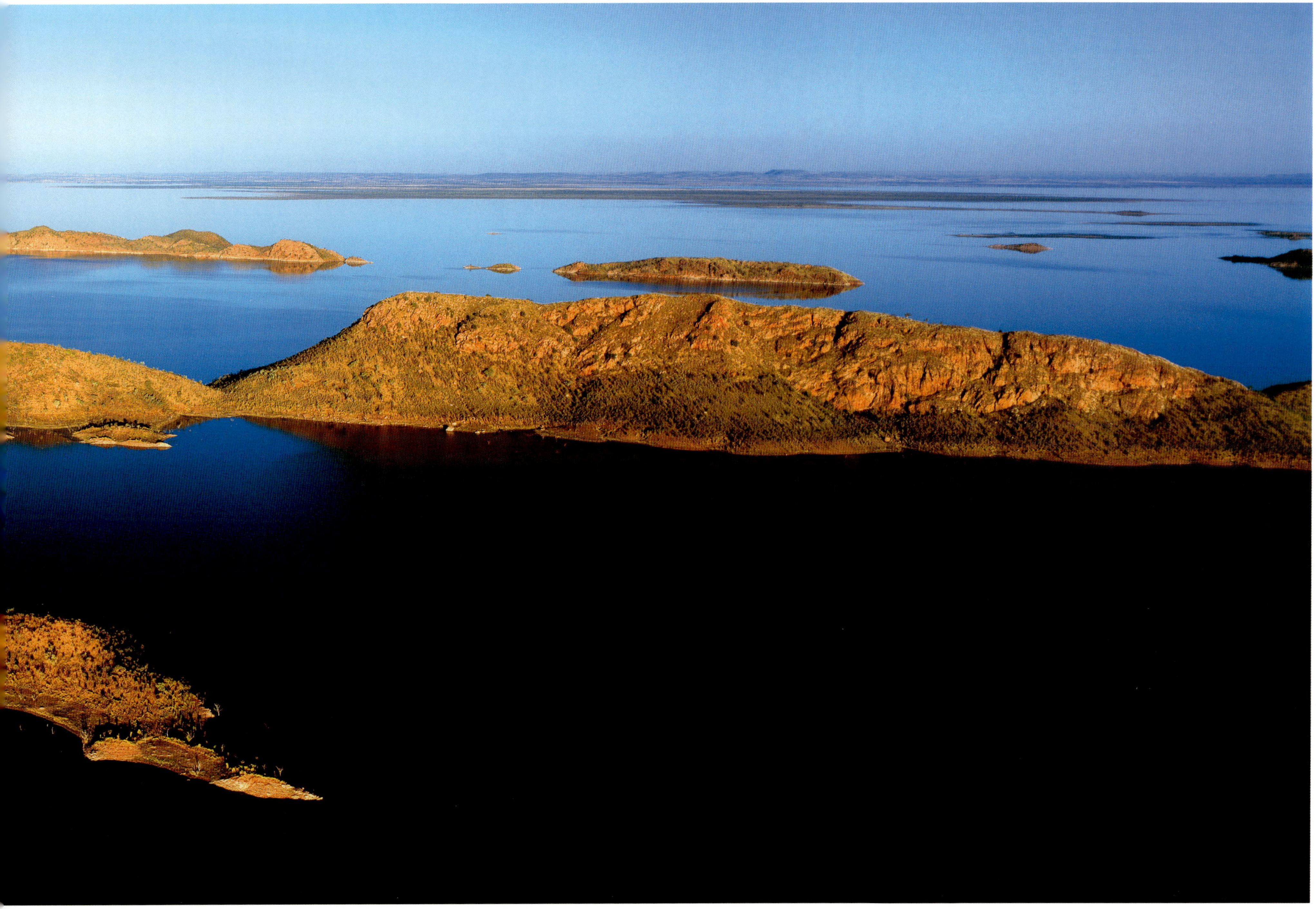

92 Mitchell Falls, Mitchell Plateau, West Kimberley

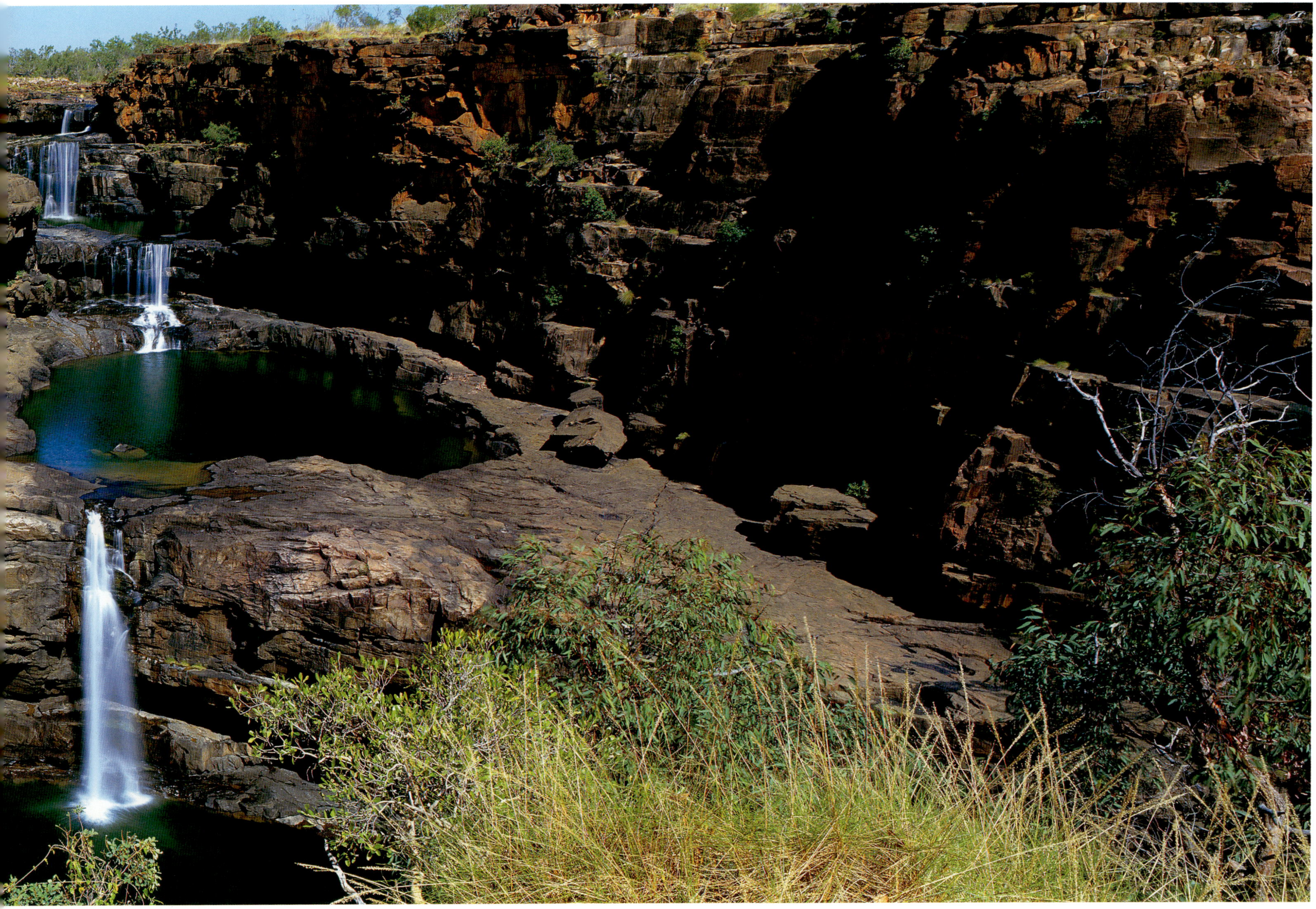

94 Sunset Boabs, Karunjie Road, El Questro Wilderness Park, East Kimberley

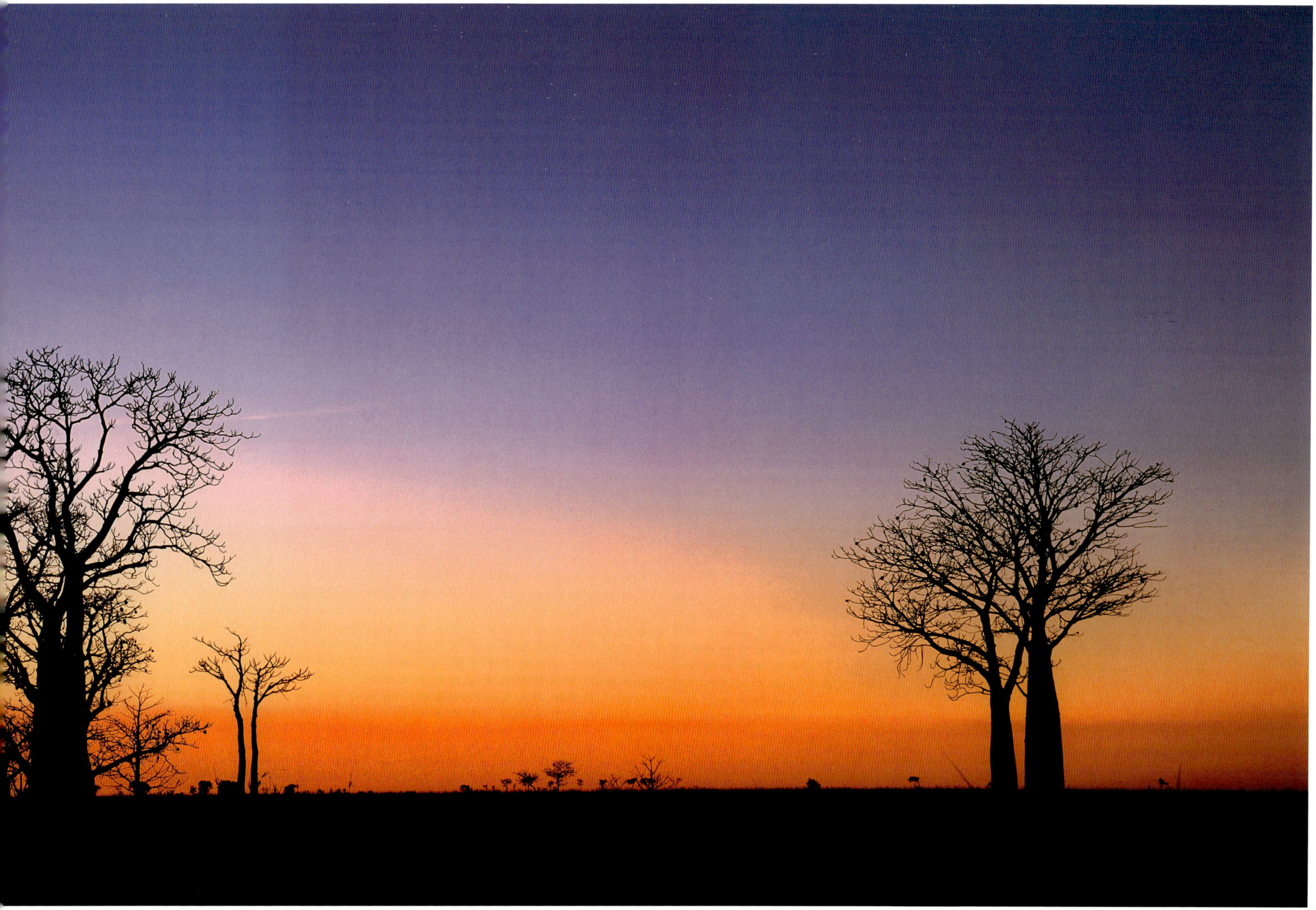

96   Galvin Gorge, Mt Barnett Station, Gibb River Road, East Kimberley

97

98 Miners Pool, Drysdale River Station, Gibb River Road, East Kimberley

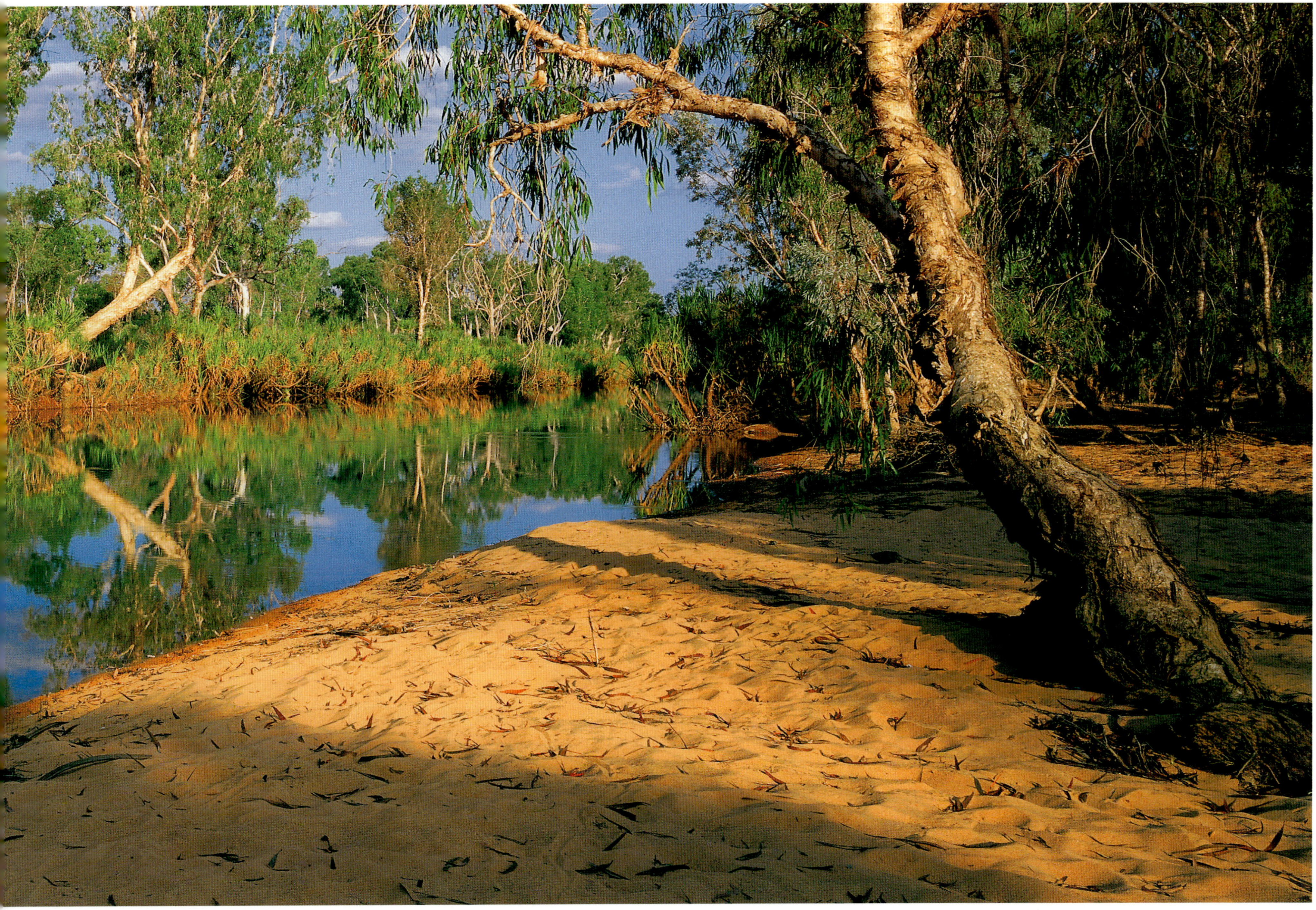

100 Aboriginal Dreamtime Statues, Wyndham, West Kimberley

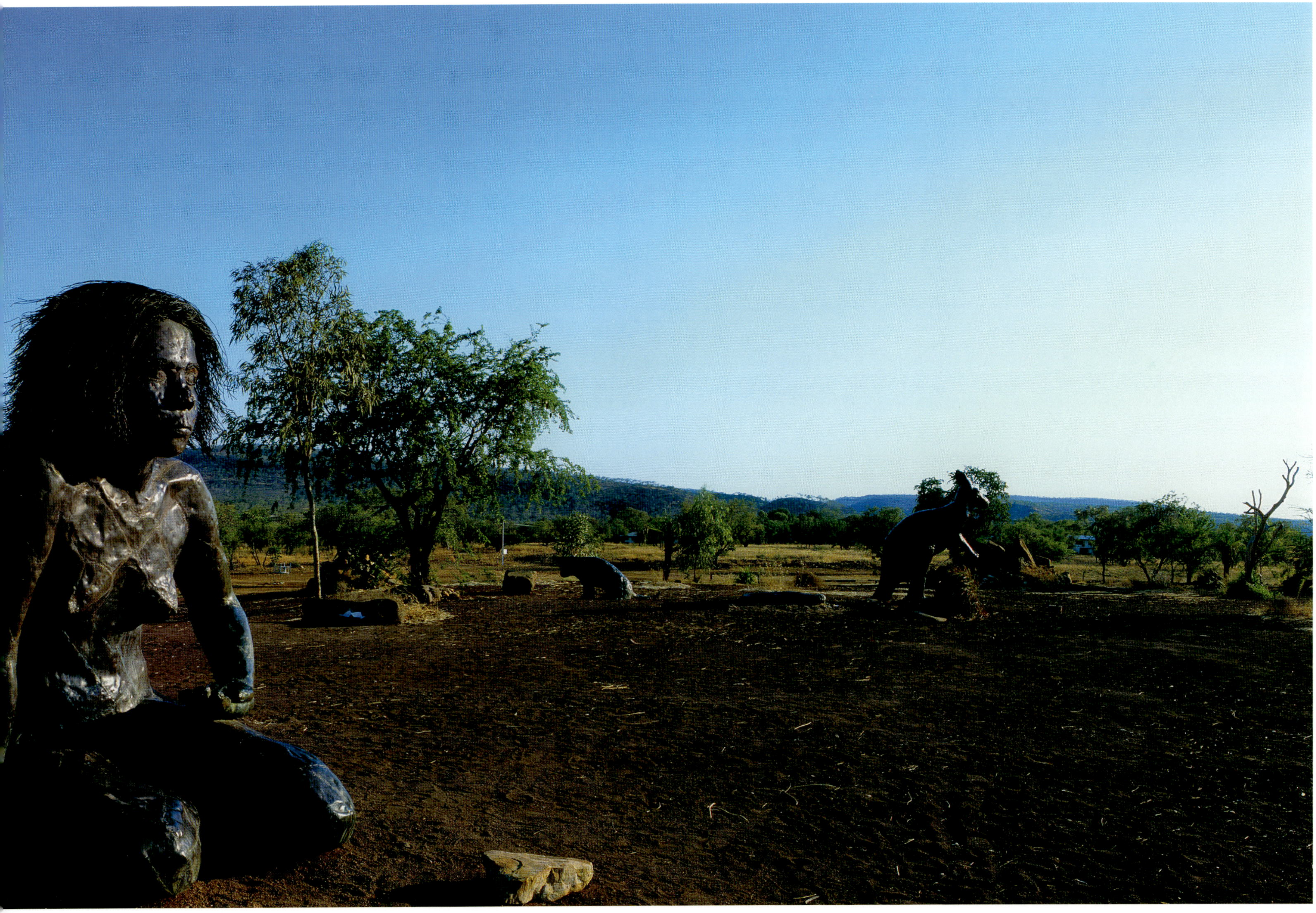

102 Bell Gorge reflections, Gibb River Road, West Kimberley

Top of Bell Gorge Falls, Gibb River Road, West Kimberley

104 Bell Gorge, Gibb River Road, West Kimberley

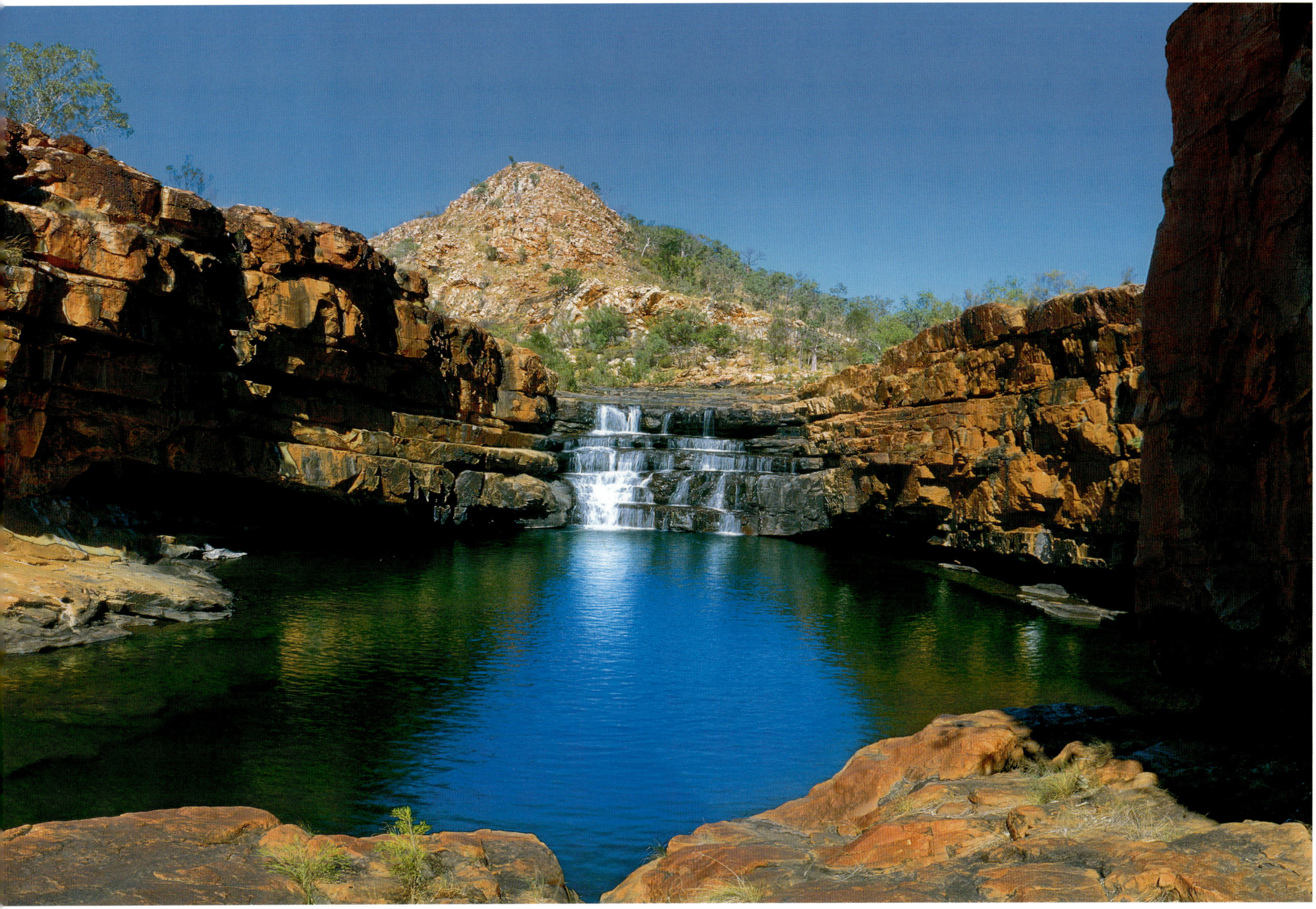

106 Relaxing on Bindoola Creek, Home Valley Station, Gibb River Road, East Kimberley

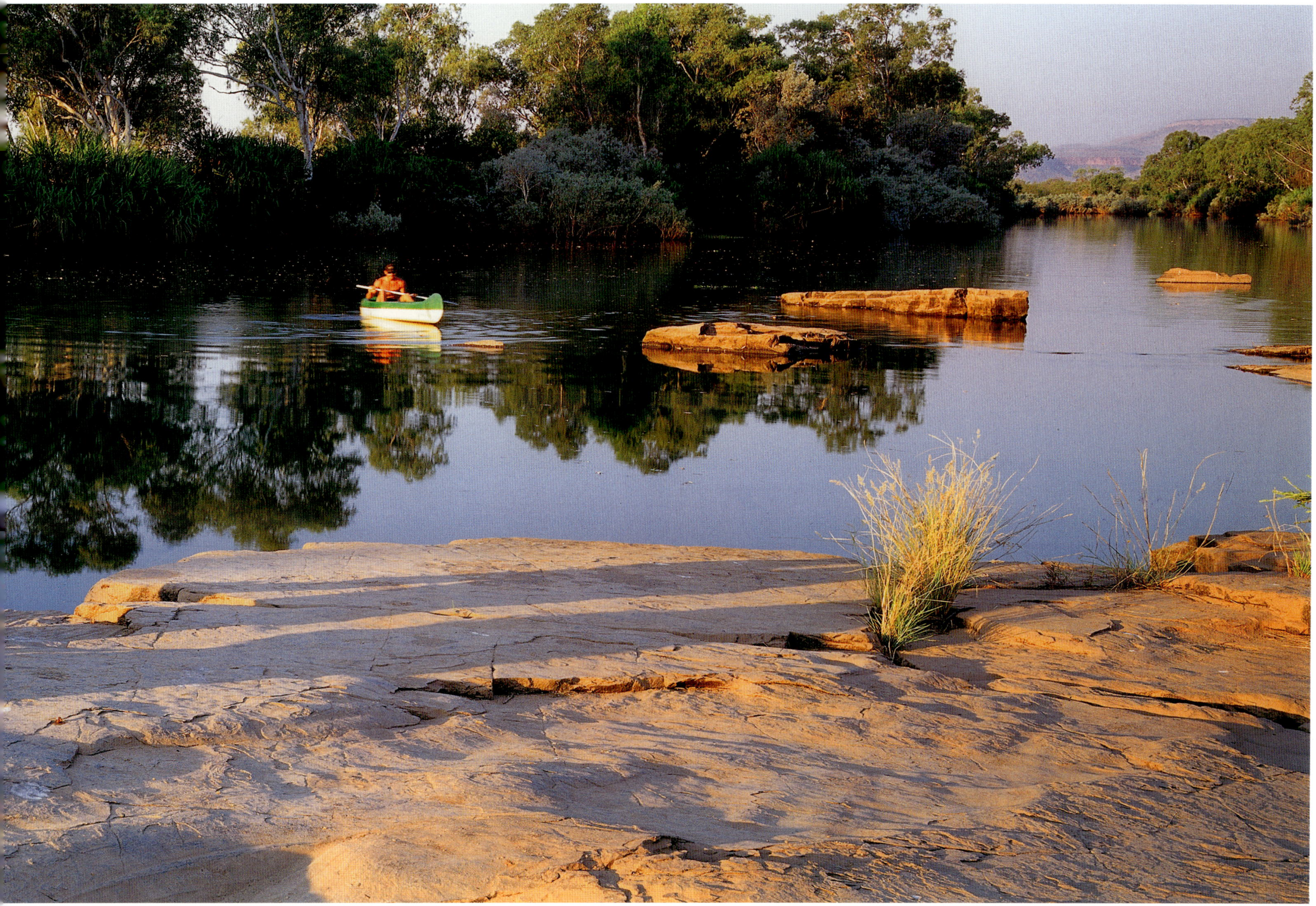

108 Cockburn Range at last light, Gibb River Road, East Kimberley

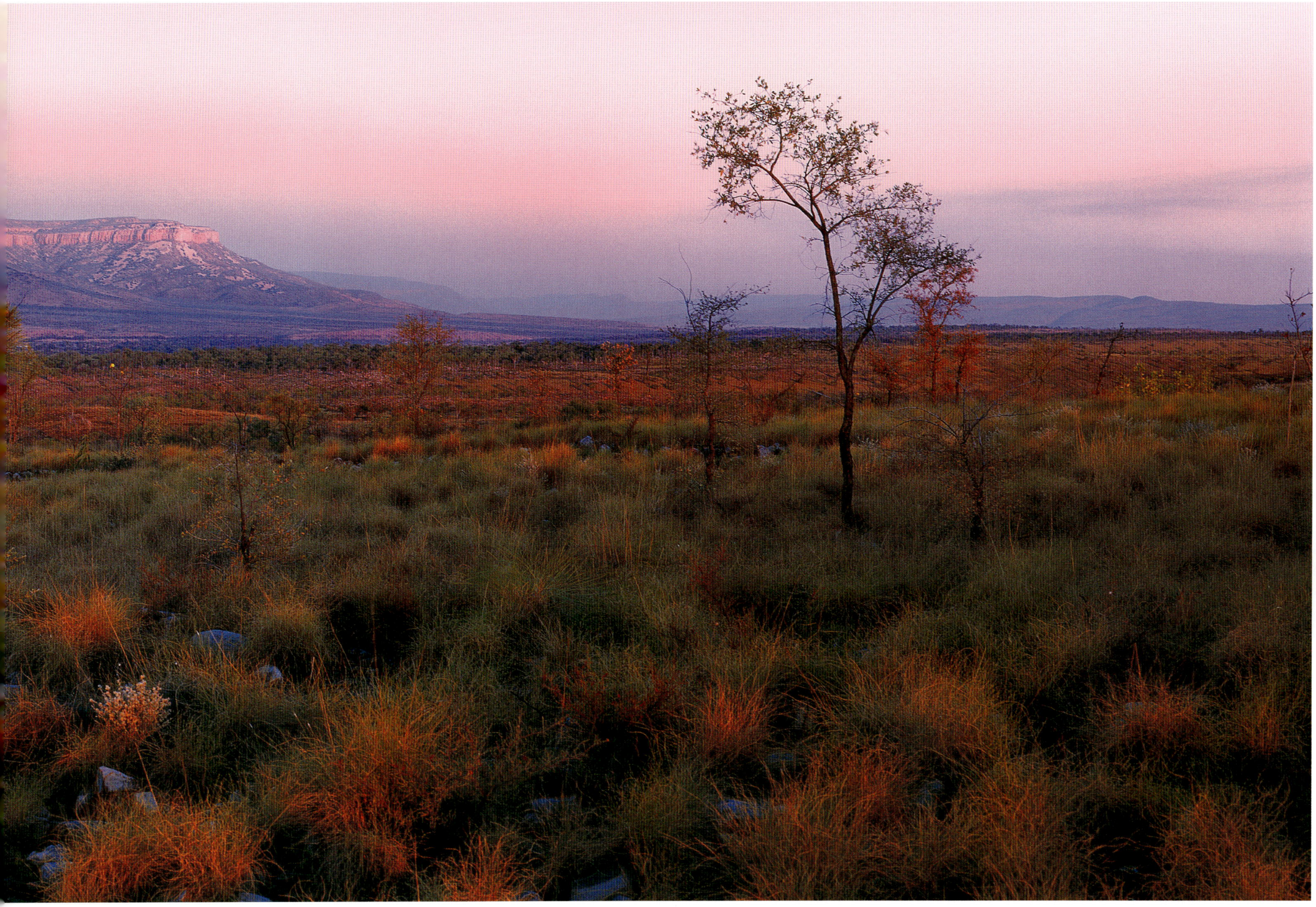

110 Imintji Store, Gibb River Road, West Kimberley

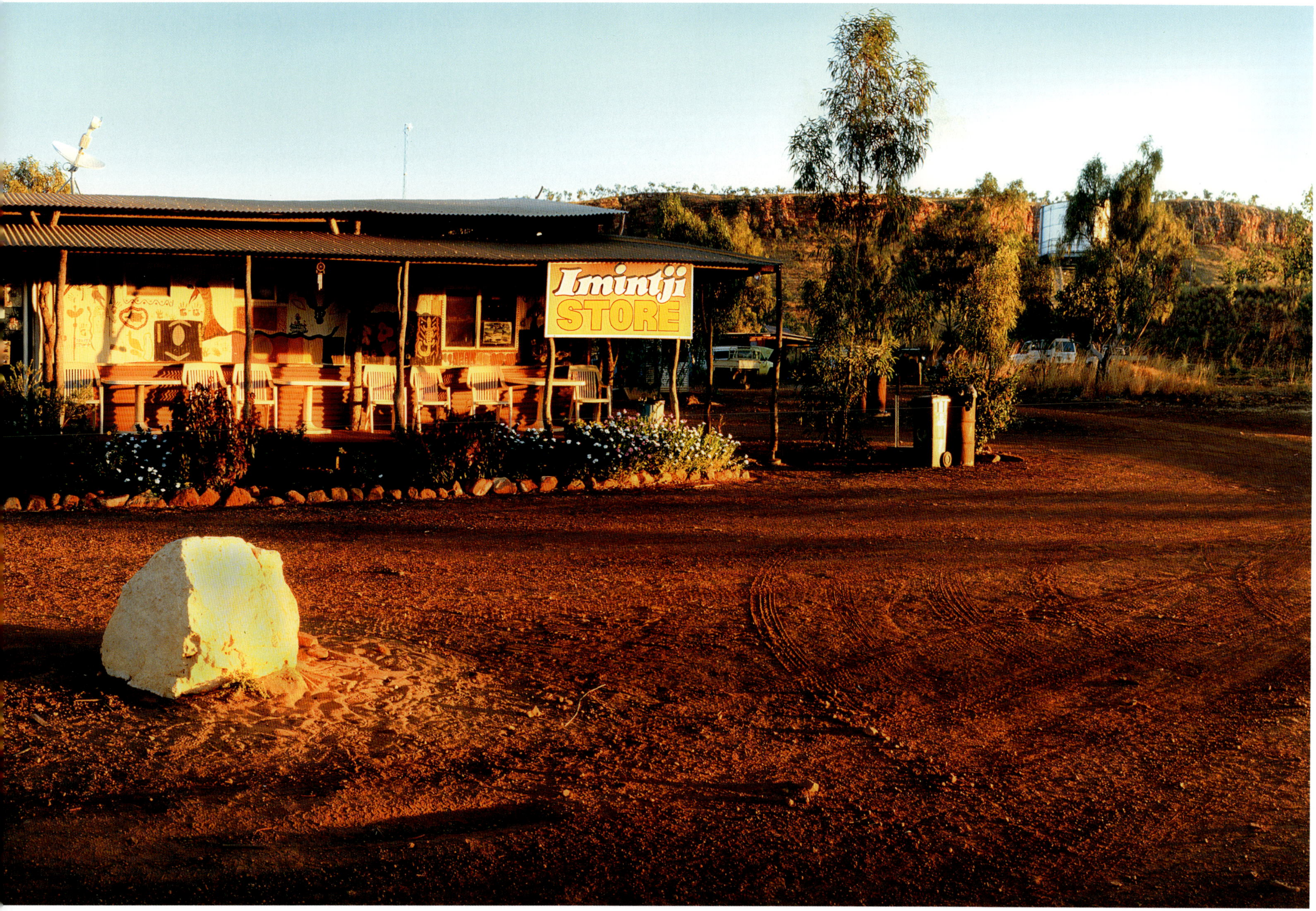
Imintji
STORE

112 Blue-winged Kookaburra, El Questro Wilderness Park, East Kimberley

A lone boab tree remote on the Kimberley Coast with the initials CD '57 remains a mystery

114 Some of the most remote beaches in the world can be found on the Kimberley coast.

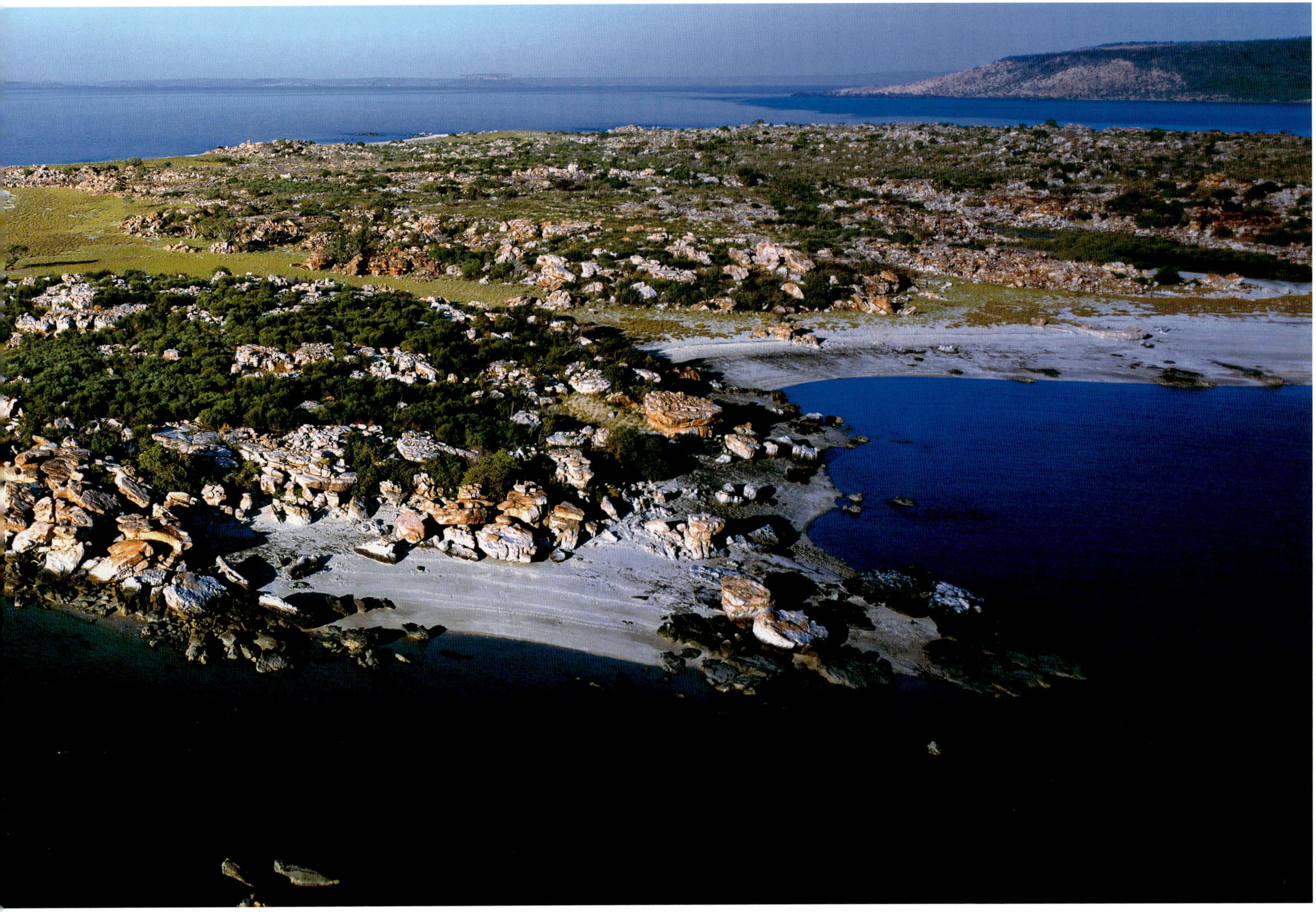

116 Heli-mustering on Mt Elizabeth Station (who often still use horses in suitable terrain)

Hessian wing walls that bluff the cattle are set up to funnel them into transportable yards 117

118 When the cattle are all in the holding yard the drafting begins.....

119

120 Lower Mitchell River Falls, Mitchell Plateau, West Kimberley

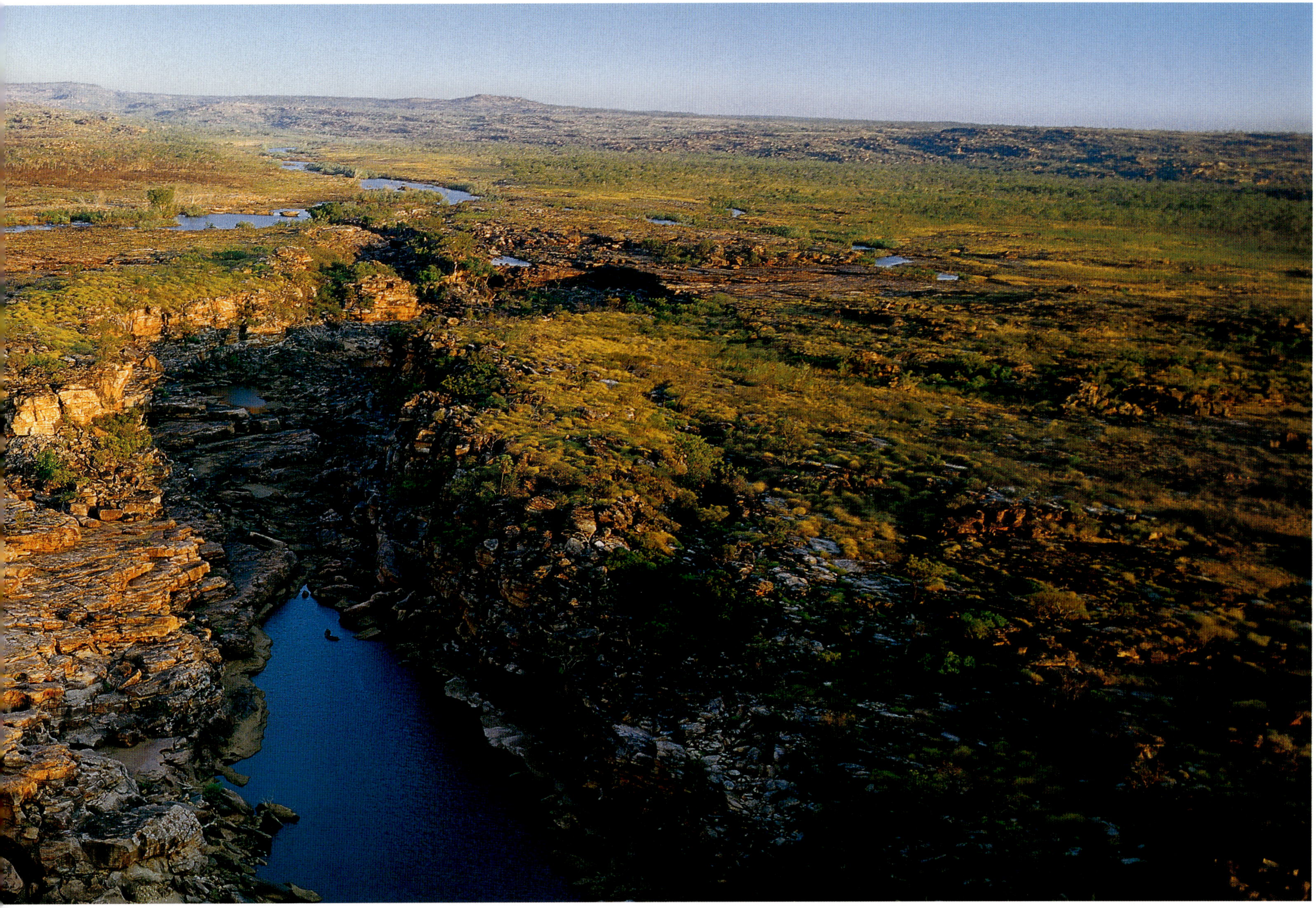

122 Branco's Lookout, El Questro Wilderness Park, East Kimberley

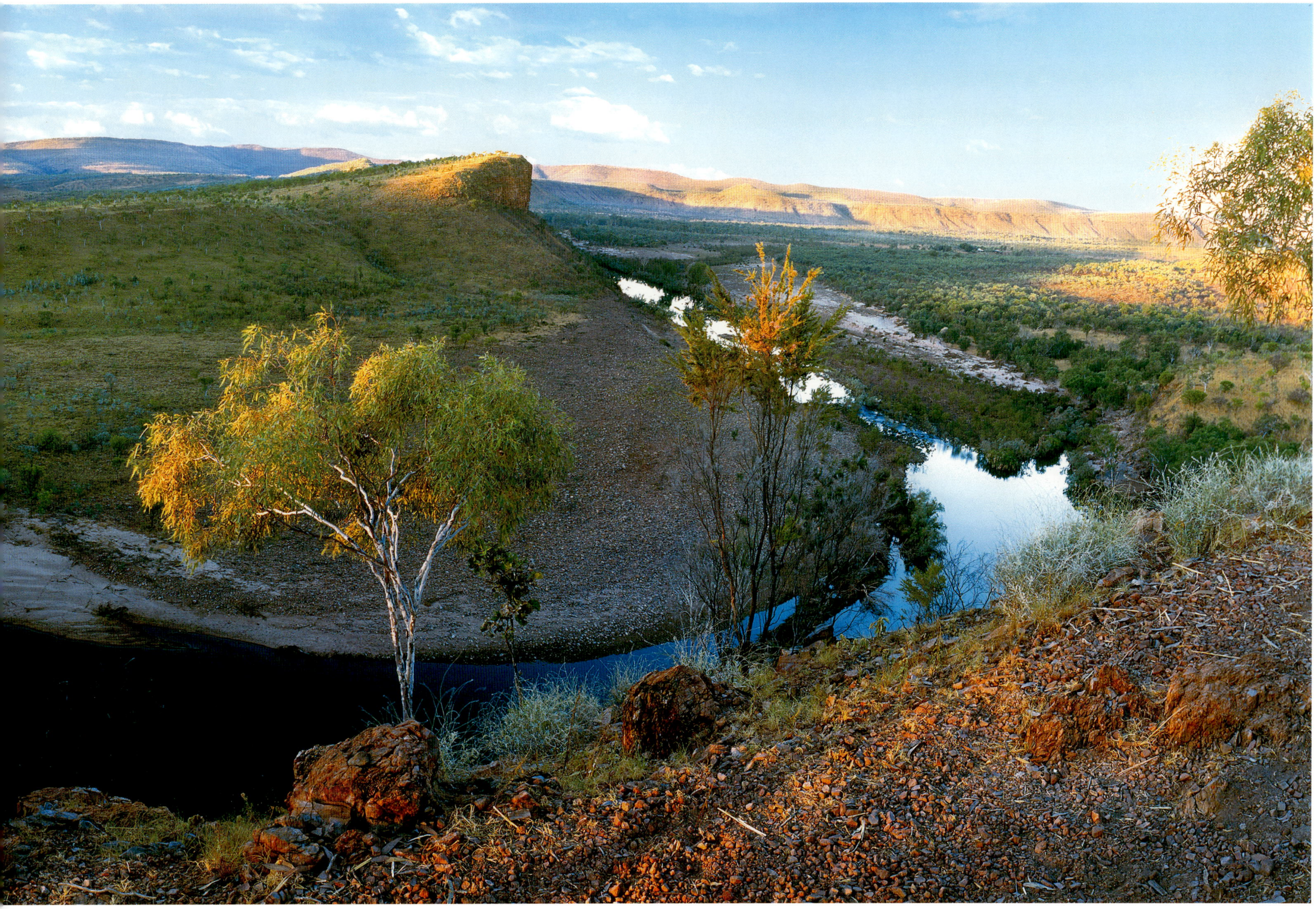

124 Lennard Gorge, Gibb River Road, West Kimberley

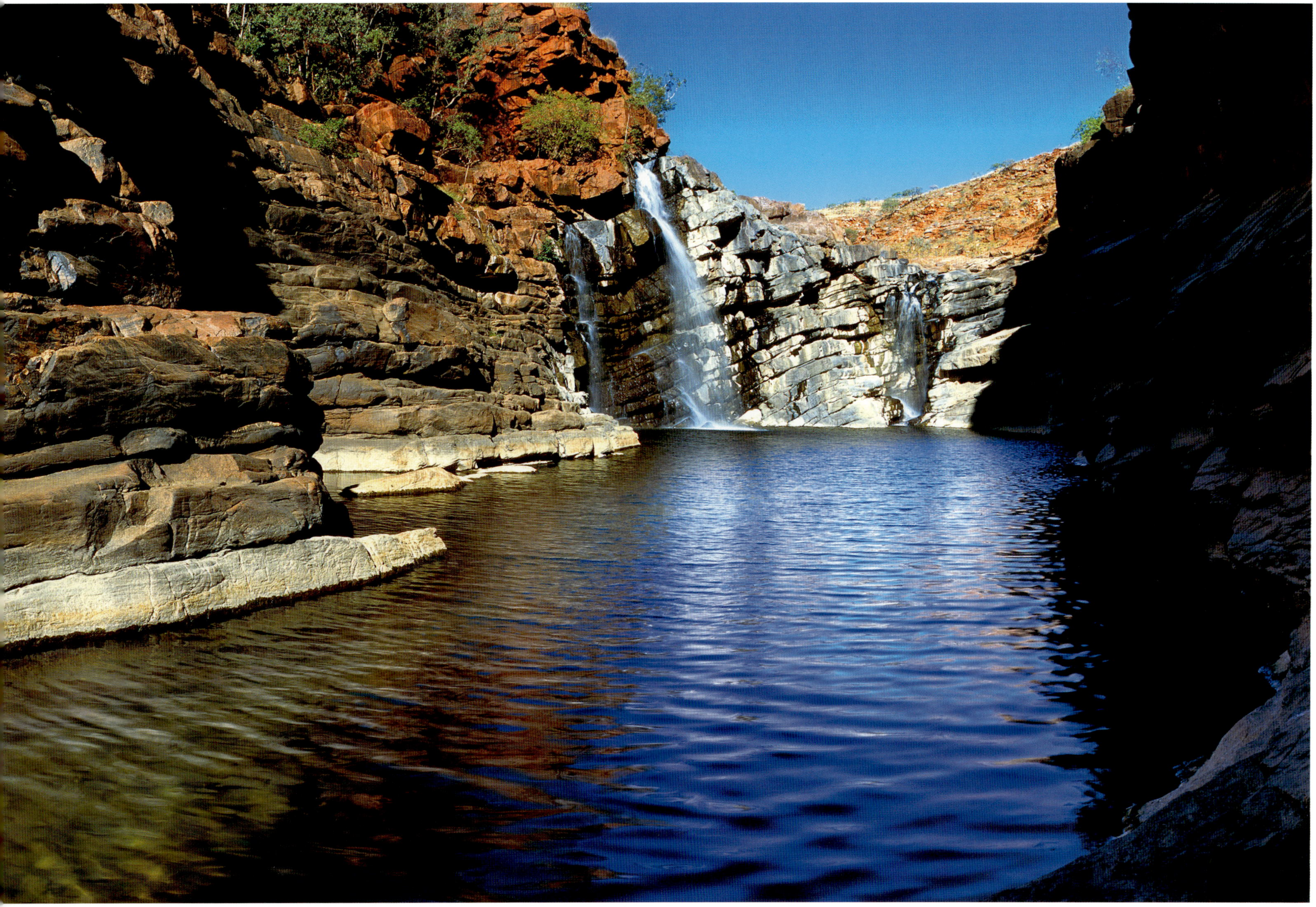

126 Windjana Gorge National Park, Gibb River Road, West Kimberley

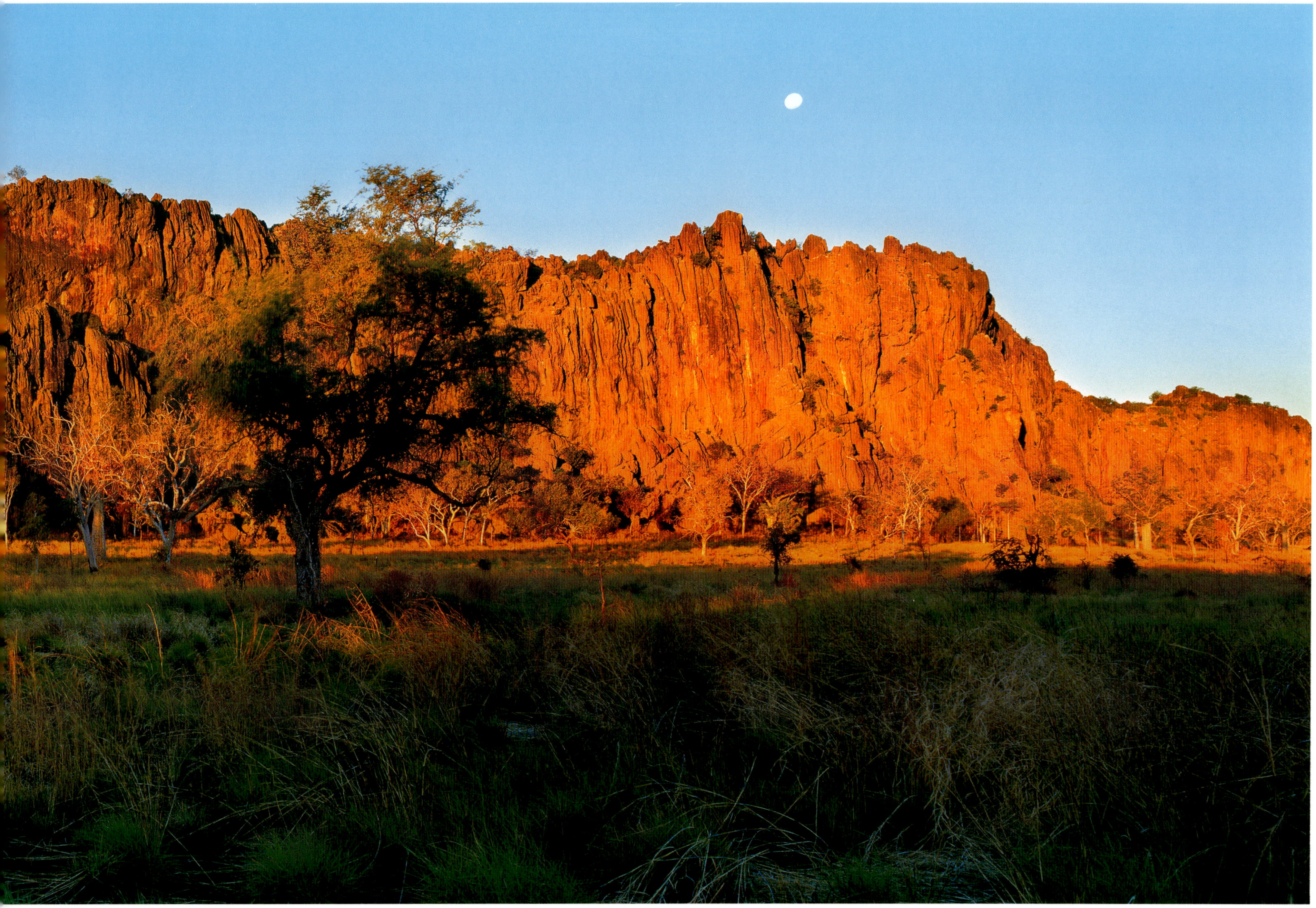

128 Wyndham Lookout, East Kimberley

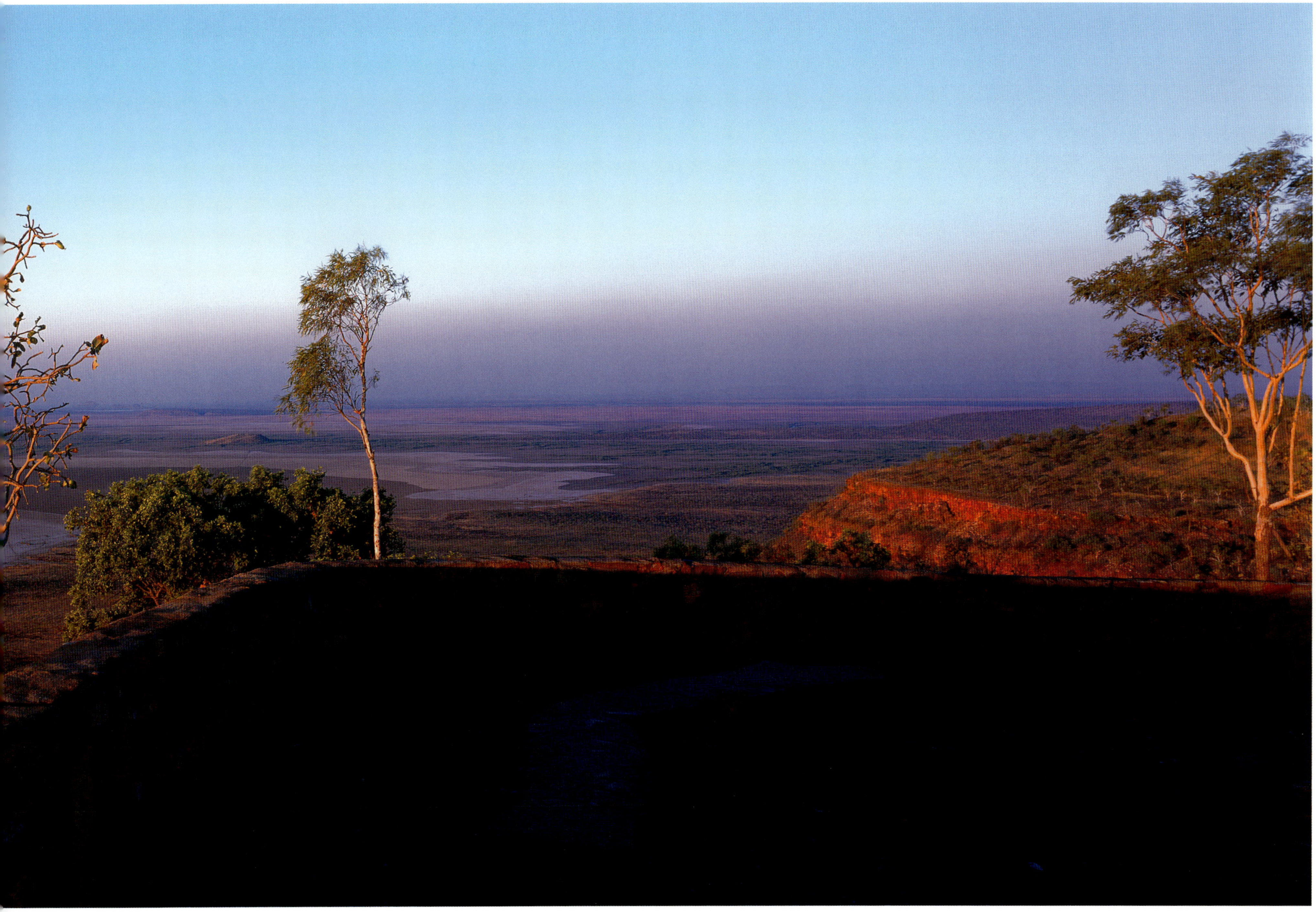

130 Zebedee Springs, El Questro Wilderness Park, East Kimberley

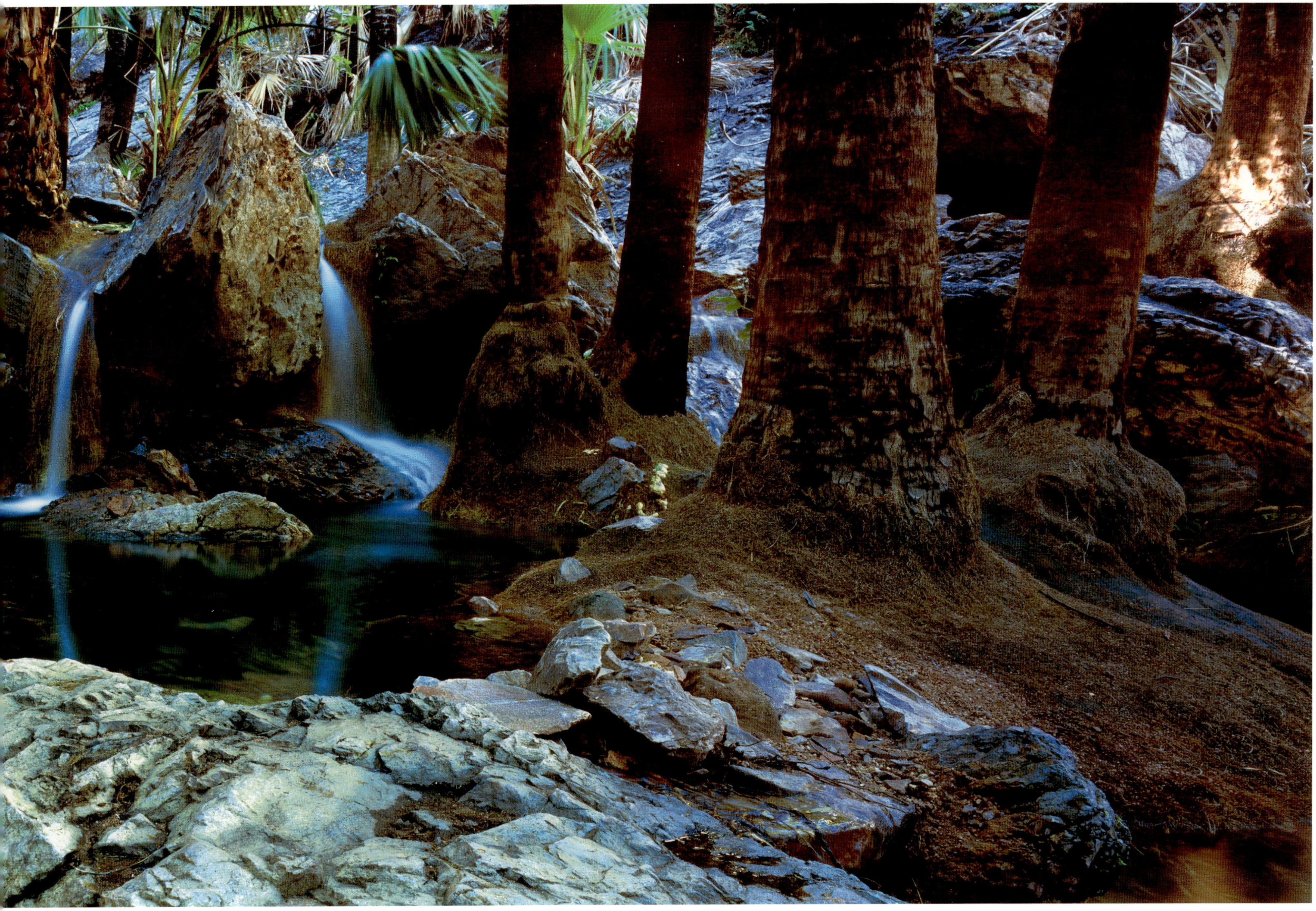

132   Boabs at Dusk, Karunjie Road, El Questro Wilderness Park, East Kimberley

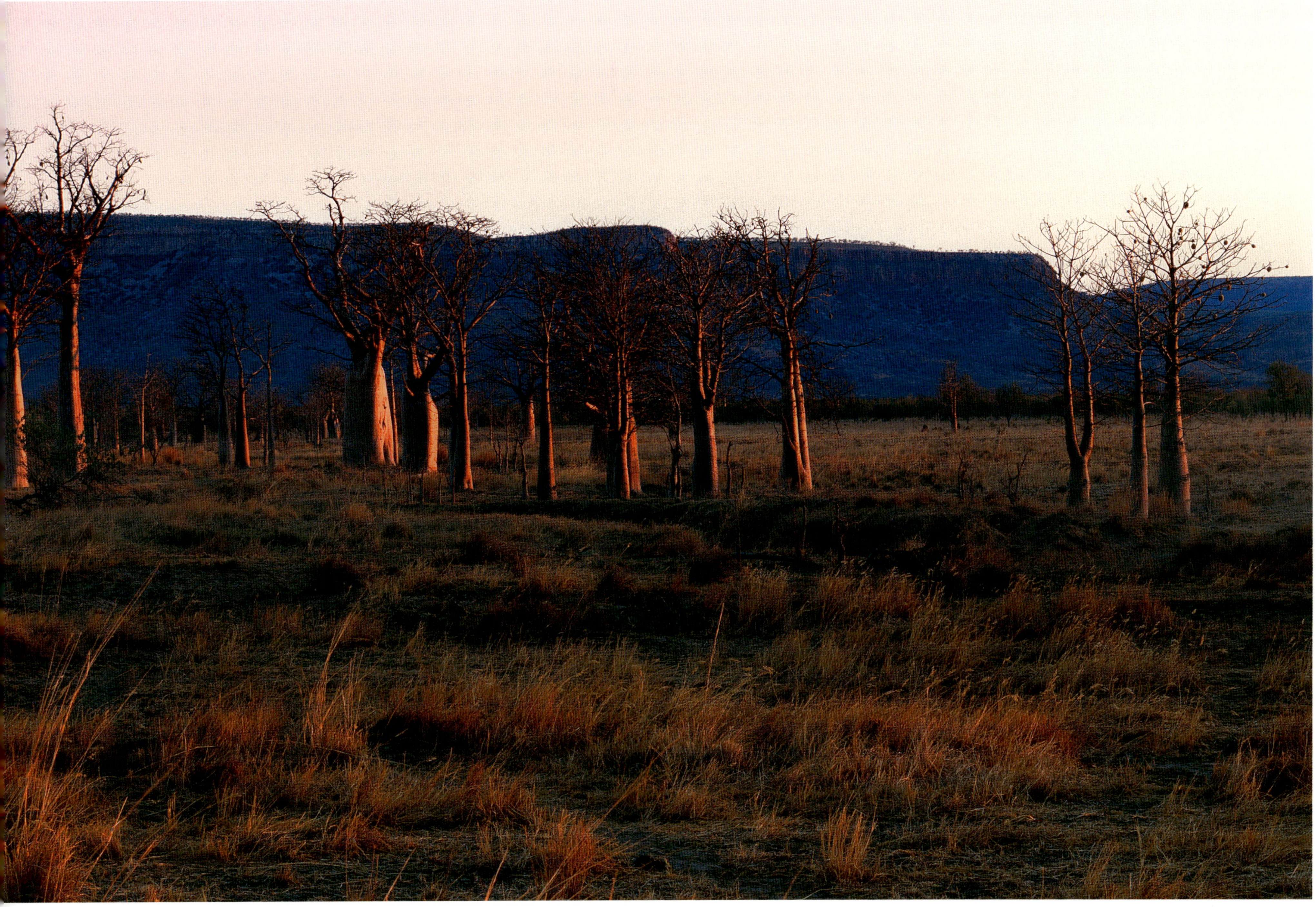

Cockburn Range, El Questro Wilderness Park, East Kimberley

Elephant Rock, Kununurra, East Kimberley

136 Natural 'China Wall', Halls Creek, East Kimberley

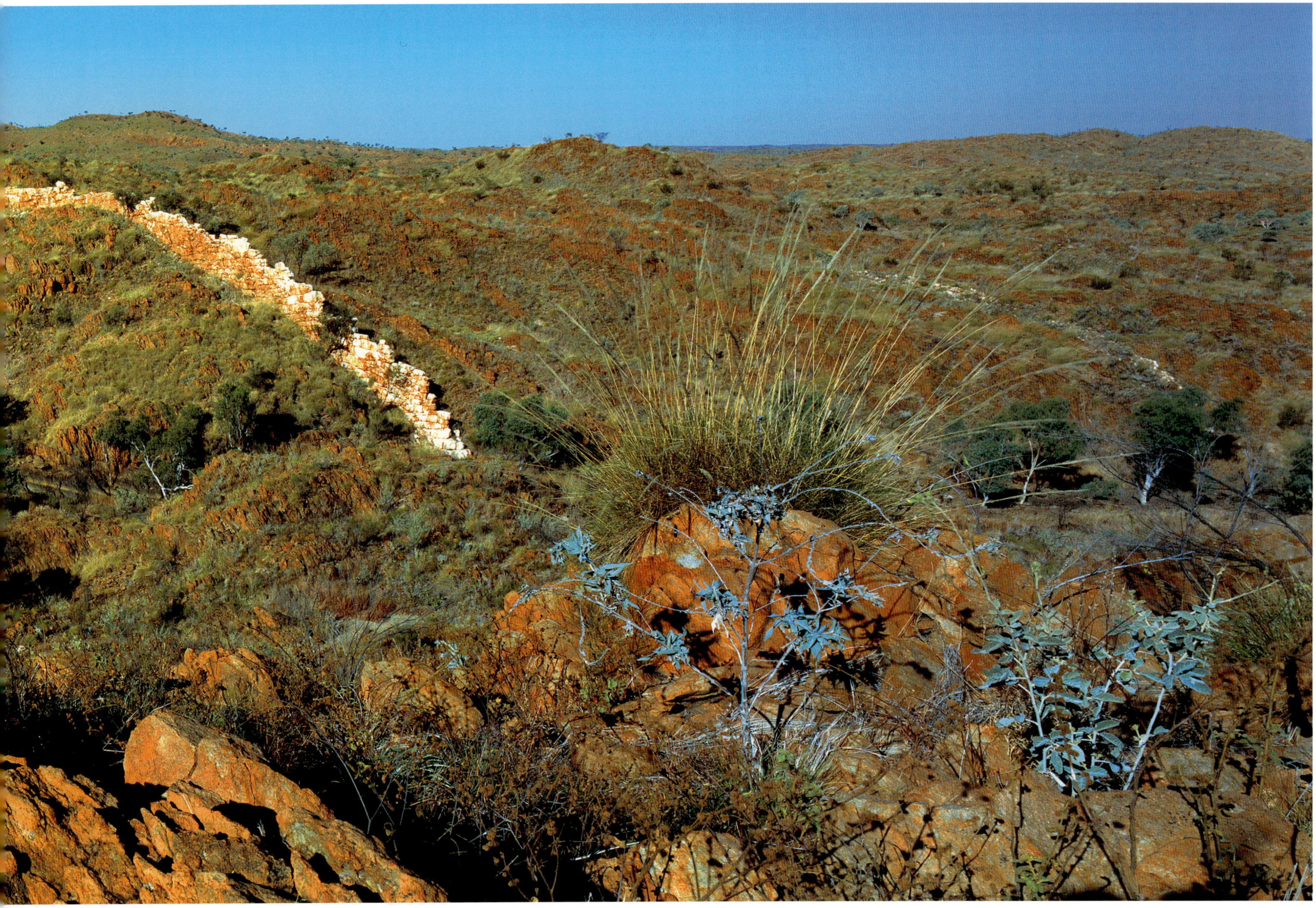

138 Pentecost River Crossing and the Cockburn Range, Gibb River Road, East Kimberley

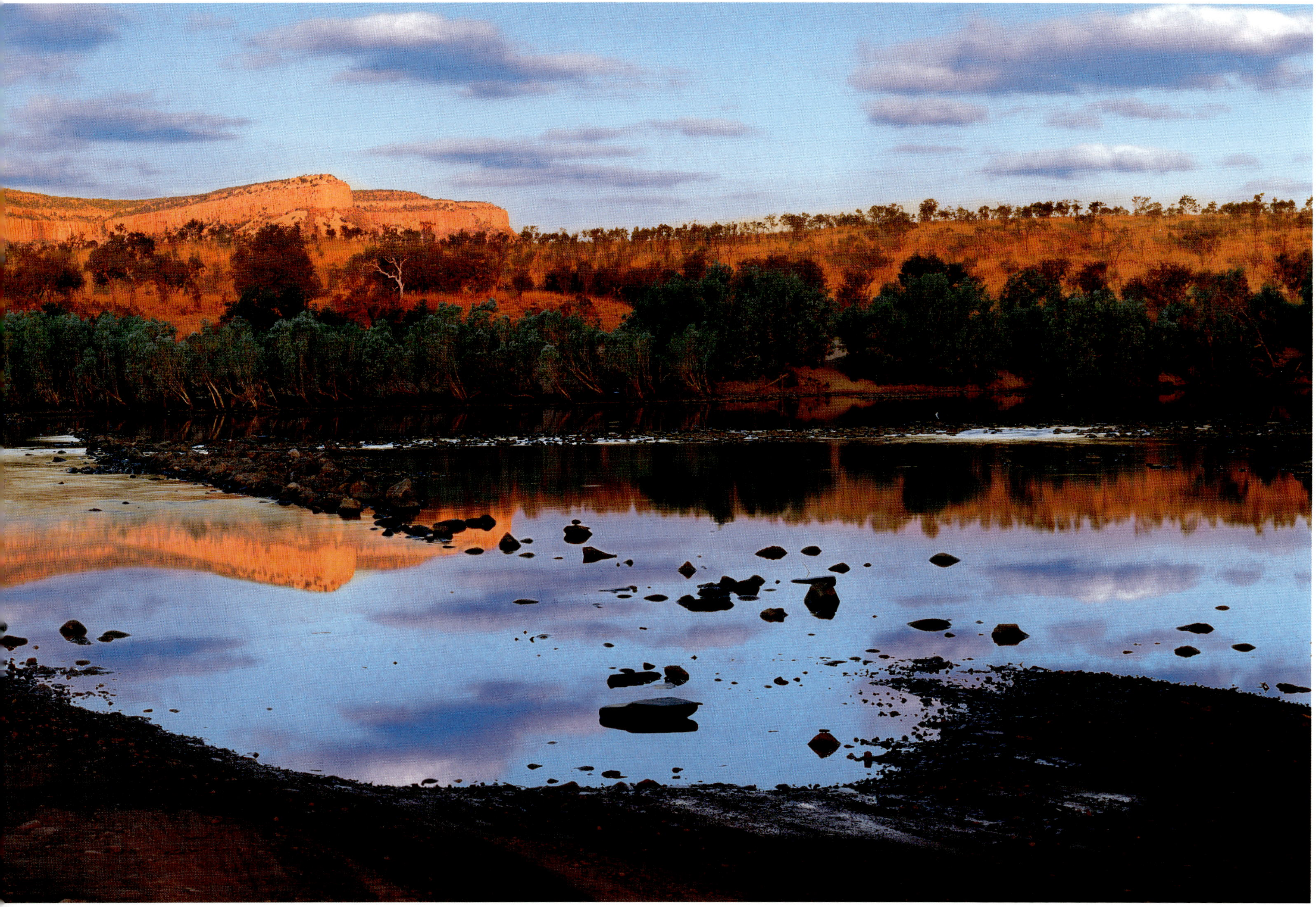

140 Emma Gorge Falls, El Questro Wilderness Park, East Kimberley

141

142 Paul Koeyers going bull catching, Drysdale River Station, Gibb River Road

Brett Lacy halter breaking a yearling on Mt Elizabeth Station 143

144 Turquoise Pool, Emma Gorge, El Questro Wilderness Park, East Kimberley

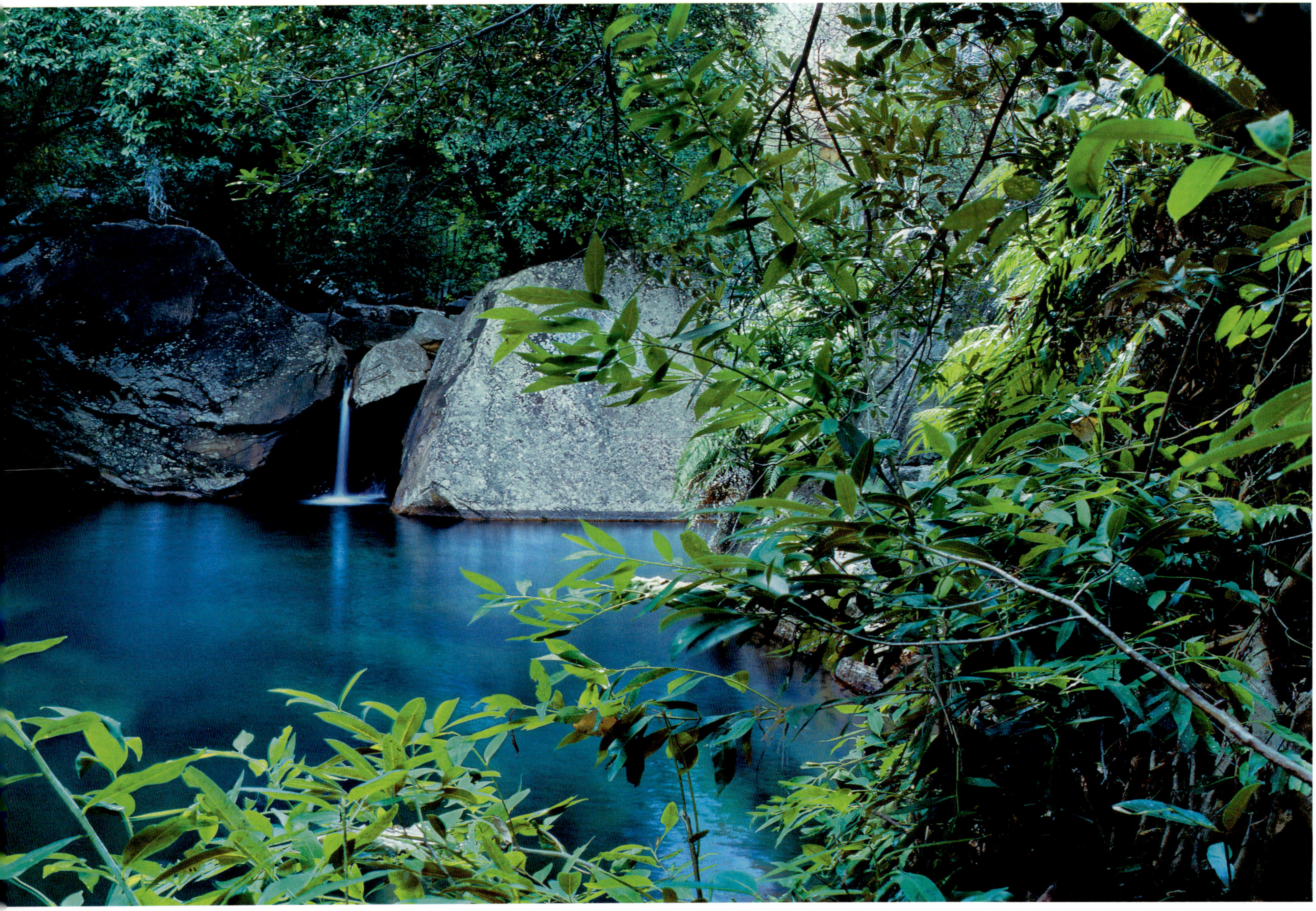

146 Geikie Gorge National Park, Kimberley

Geikie Gorge National Park, Kimberley

148 Geikie Gorge National Park, Kimberley

Geikie Gorge National Park, Kimberley 149

150 McGowan's Island beach, Kalumburu Coast, Kimberley

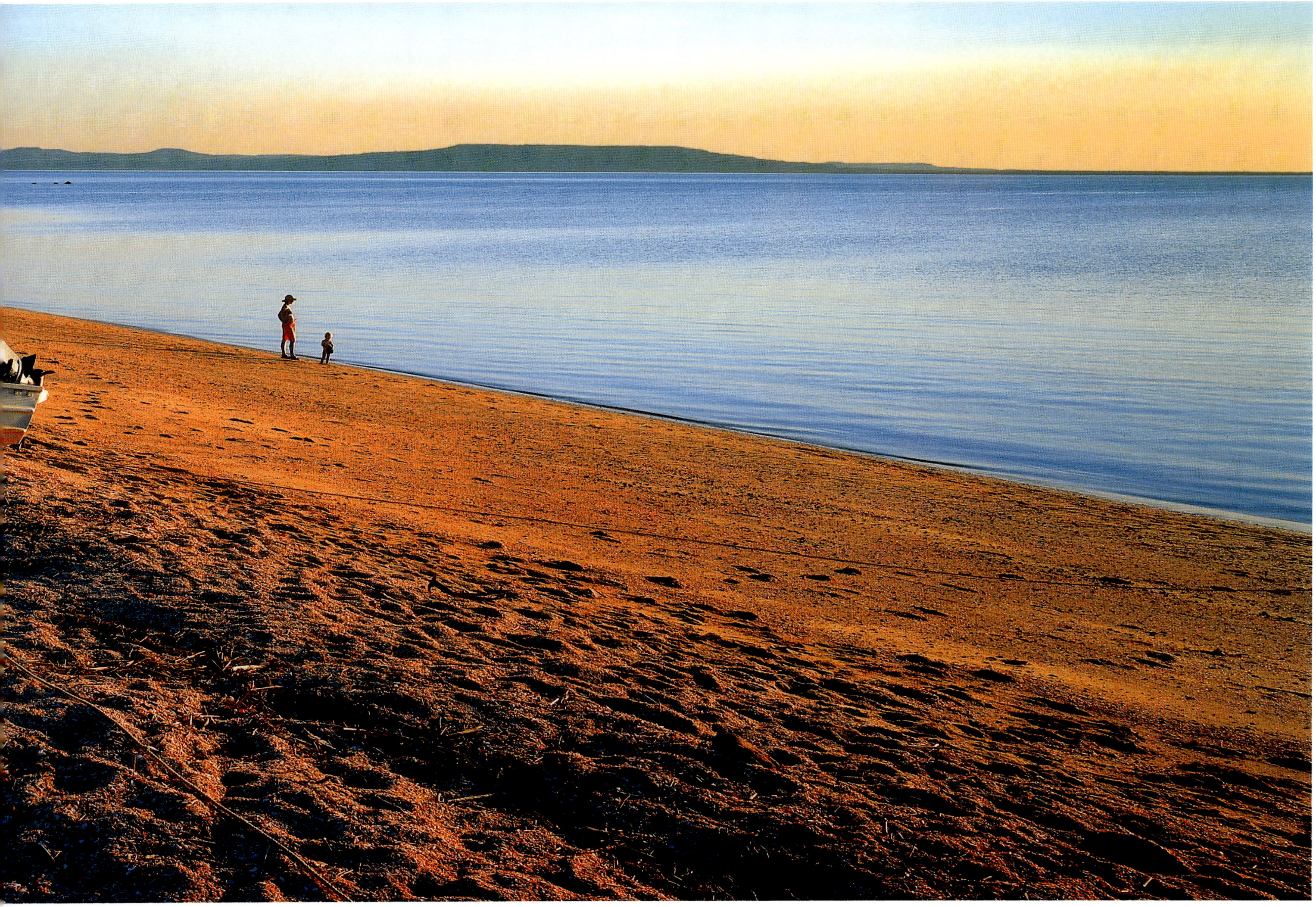

152 Legendary adventurer / film maker, Malcom Douglas, at home at his crocodile park in Broome.

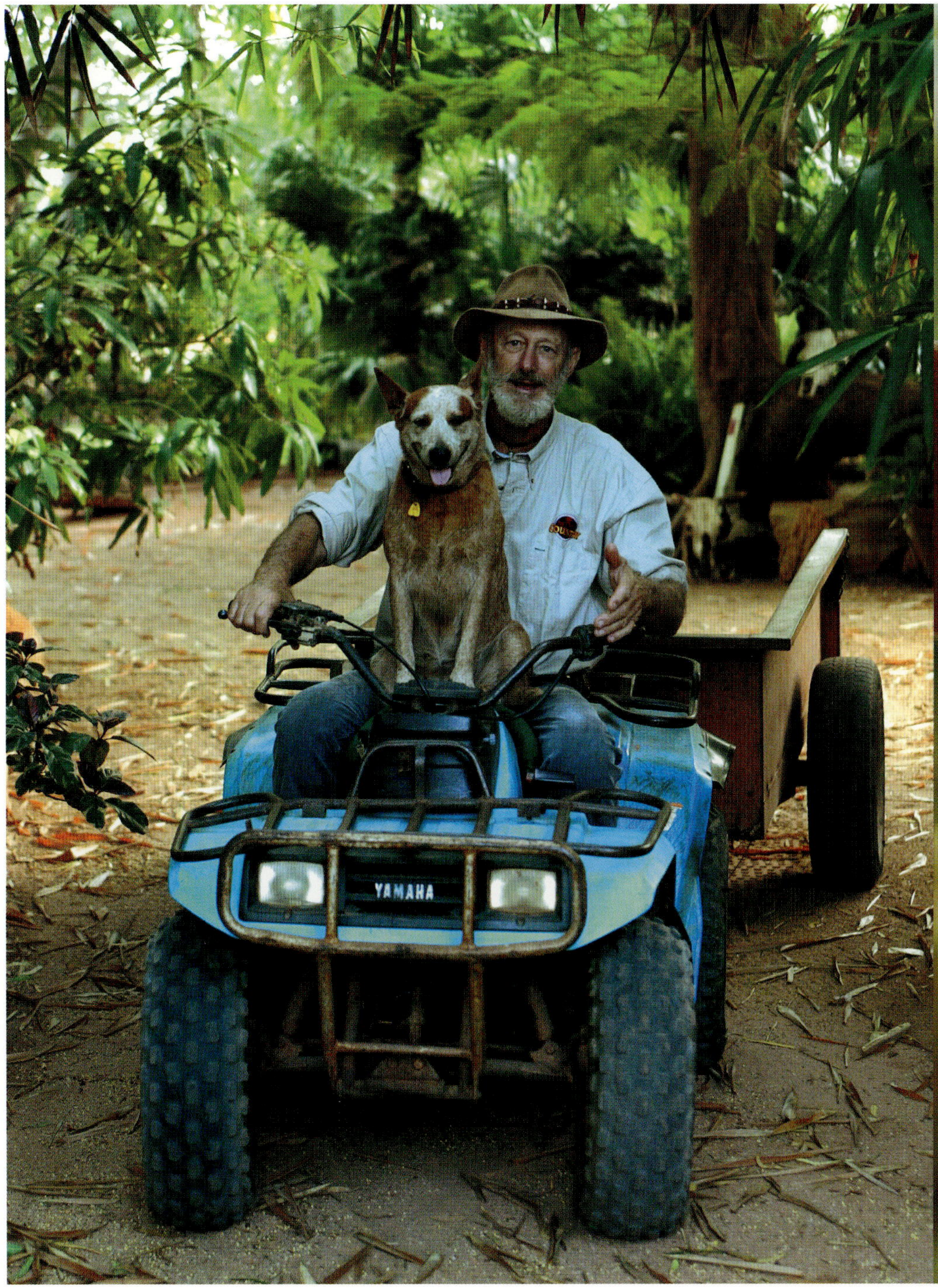
YAMAHA

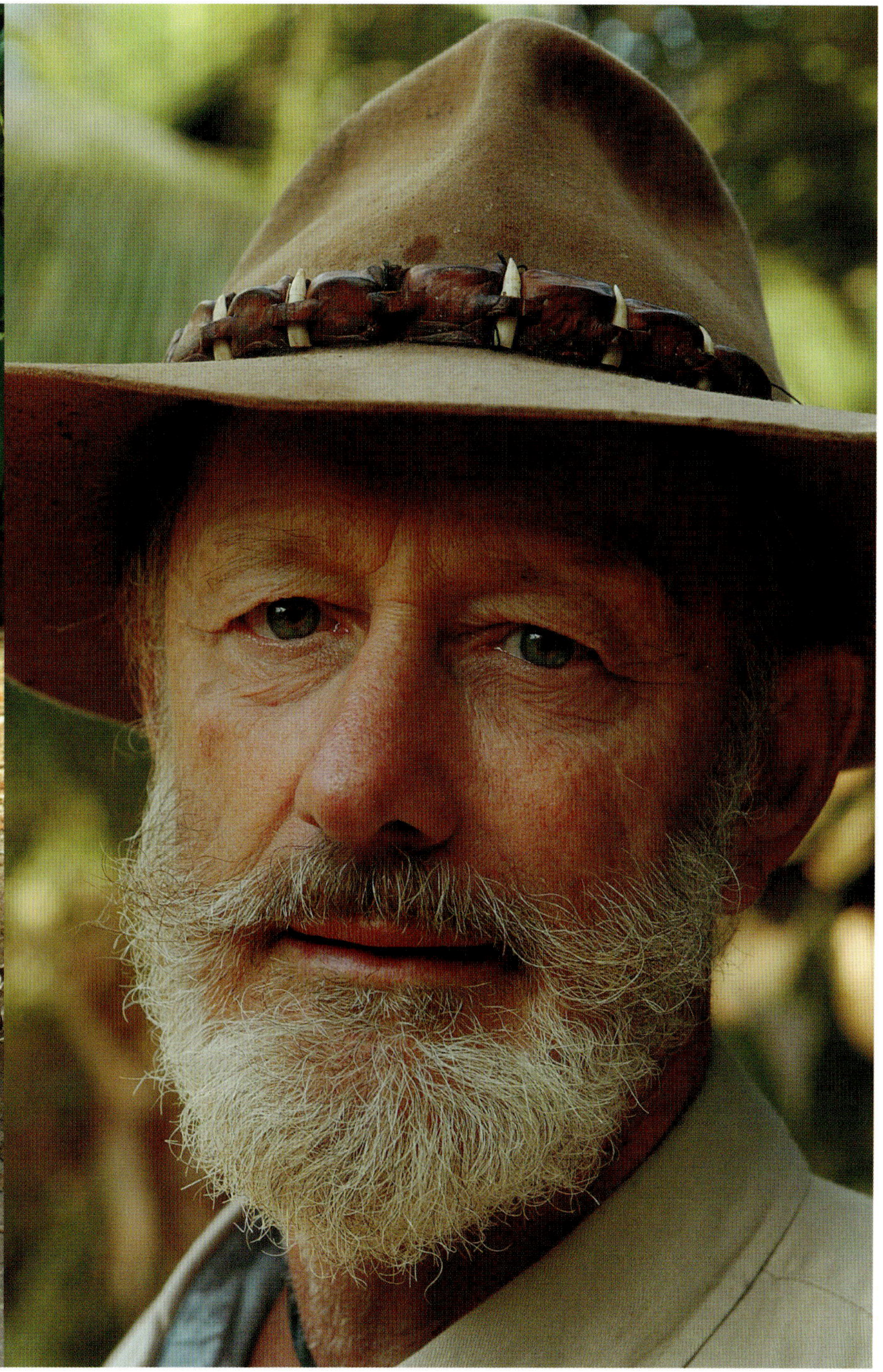

154 Dimond Gorge, Mornington Wildlife Sanctuary, Kimberlery

Dimond Gorge situated on the Fitzroy River is part of the Mornington Wildlife Sanctuary. It is owned and operated by the Australian Wildlife Conservancy (AWC). AWC is an independent, non profit organization dedicated to the conservation of Australia's threatened wildlife. AWC has 10 wildlife sanctuaries around Australia. Their operations are funded primarily by tax deductible donations.

156 The luxurious El Questro Homestead on Chamberlin Gorge

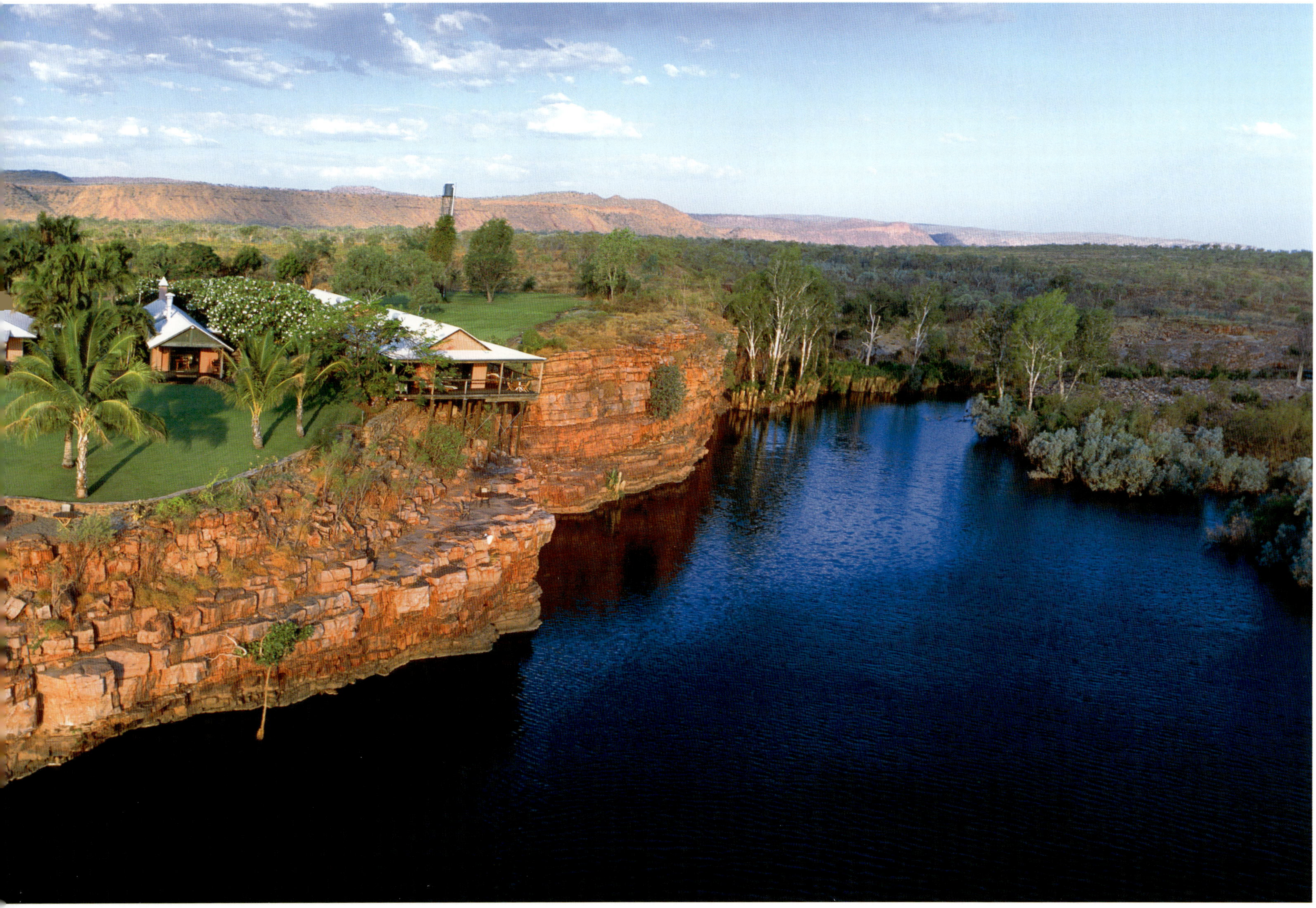

PHOTOGRAPHER'S NOTES:
The photograph of the Cable Beach sunset on this page (a cropped version) was taken by a friend of mine Yani Sotiroski, a Broome local. He had never previously taken a professional photo. His basic knowledge of shutter speed, aperture, focus and metering along with local knowledge helped Yani capture God's spectacular creation.

It is important in landscape photography to put in the time to get to know an area well at different times of the day and in different seasons. You never know when some magic might happen or perhaps only when it is more likely to occure.

Ask any pilot in the Kimberley just how fast the light fades when the sun is on the horizon and I'm sure they'll tell you it's black before you know it, especially when compared to the Northern Territory. I found shooting in the late afternoon light, known as "the magic hour", to be more like fifteen minutes. Sunrises brighten to less desirable high contrast light just as fast. Common bush fire smoke on the horizon can often turn the soft warm light to overcast grey. Along with the wind, I found photographing the Kimberley in the dry season to be very challenging. The shot on the cover perhaps appeals a great deal more to me than others.... I was just about to pack up due to the smoke when the sun half broke through creating the surreal glow for less than a minute around the same time the Jabiru in the nest stood up...... Thank you God.

Film can be quite inaccurate in certain conditions. To make photographs more true to life I sometimes use filters to pull down bright skies and to correct the colour temperature. To learn how film sees takes a bit of practice. I still waist a lot of film getting shots to look accurate. I mainly use Fuji Provia 100F for its more realistic colour it has over a wider range of lighting conditions. I use Fuji Velvia in situations where I need to preserve contrast where the difference in colour is more subtle.

The step across to panoramic photography for me was a nightmare at first and often still is.... Being so wide it is amazing how your own shadow gets in the way. These camera's don't just use film they eat it!.... Four shots to a 120 roll. Bending light accurately onto such a large film plane requires expensive optics for realistic colour and sharpness. Being so wide some lenses need centre graduate filters to even up the exposure which you then have to compensate for. Along with using small apertures for good depth of field and fine grain film (slow speed), often makes it difficult to get fast shutter speeds...... If the wind is around it can produce undesirable results such as blurred trees, grass, water reflections and so on. To me this all just adds to the fulfillment when I sometimes get a shot that I can actually use.

I feel so privileged to have been born and raised in this great land and to have travelled extensively with my parents from an early age. The natural beauty of Western Australia inspired me to learn photography and not for a second will I ever take it for granted.

Cable Beach sunset, Broome

I would like to offer my sincere thanks to the following companies for their assistance in recent years. Without their support this book would not have been possible.

Heliwork WA

Slingair

www.slingair.com.au
1800 095 500
Kununurra W.A.

PLAZA DIGITAL CAMERA • VIDEO

www.plazacameras.com.au
1800 804 041
Perth W.A.

Western Australia's North Pilbara and the Kimberley
Ben Knapinski
First published 2003
By Envisage Publishing
Maps designed by Jonathan Davies

National Library of Australia
ISBN 0-9750614-0-2

Proudly **PRINTED IN AUSTRALIA**
Printed by Lamb Print
Perth, W.A.

Copyright photography and text
©Ben Knapinski

All rights reserved. No part of this publication may be reproduced, stored in a retrieval system or transmitted in any form or by any means electronic, mechanical, photocopying, recording or otherwise without the prior written permission of the publisher and copyright holder.

VISIT THE BEN KNAPINSKI OUTBACK WILDERNESS GALLERY ONLINE:

www.bjk.com.au

Zebedee Springs, El Questro Wilderness Park

160 Some of the Kimberley characters that I had the privilege of meeting along the way.